TUTORING TOOTERS

A Group Recorder Method

Shirley W. McRae

MICHAEL D. BENNETT, Editor

MARY NORMAN, Illustrator

ISBN 0-934017-13-1

© Copyright 1990

Memphis Musicraft Publications

3149 Southern Avenue • Memphis, TN 38111

SONGS

CONTENTS

INDEX

PREFACE

Tutoring Tooters began as a short collection of soprano recorder materials for college students in elementary education programs, in which a course in music was required. Now in greatly expanded form, the book is useful for anyone with no previous musical training as an introduction to musical concepts and skills through learning to play this instrument. The book's ninety-seven activities are arranged in approximate order of difficulty but need not all be undertaken in a single course.

The approach used is perhaps unique in that, in addition to suggested accompaniments for piano and guitar, enrichment ideas are presented for those classes taught in the manner of Orff Schulwerk. While proficiency on the recorder is the primary objective of this book, games and ostinato patterns for Orff barred instruments and percussion are suggested for enrichment. These accompaniments are intentionally simple, so as not to detract from the recorder experience itself.

Numerous song texts are provided so that the melodies may be sung as well as played. The music is drawn almost entirely from international folk traditions and works of the early masters. Most of the music is equally suited to children or adult learners.

The recorder is often regarded as a means of introducing students to the pleasures of music in a social context--the group setting. I hope *Tutoring Tooters* will contribute to that happy experience, and it is therefore dedicated to tutors and tooters everywhere.

Finally, I wish to acknowledge the many contributions of my editor, Don Bennett, whose imagination and organizational skills have greatly enhanced this book. I think we are still friends.

Shirley W. McRae
Memphis, Tennessee

Dance

Czech Folksong

RHYTHM TUTOR

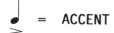

♩ = **ACCENT**

AN **ACCENT** MARK ABOVE OR BELOW A NOTE TELLS YOU TO PLAY IT WITH MORE FORCE--A PUFF OF AIR AT THE BEGINNING OF THE ARTICULATION, RATHER THAN A SMOOTH AIR FLOW. BE CAREFUL NOT TO OVERBLOW AND CAUSE AN OUT-OF-TUNE PITCH OR A SQUEAK.

GETTING READY

Practice these patterns with accents:

Slowly sight read the song. Observe the accents.

PERFORMANCE

Play the song with the piano accompaniment shown below at a lively tempo.

ENRICHMENT

Add the percussion instruments to the piano accompaniment.

FOREWORD

FEATURES

Tutor boxes highlight basic concepts in five categories: rhythm, meter, form, recorder technique, and melody.

Important terms appear initially in boldface type.

A tutor/term index makes review easy.

Chapters begin with exercises to integrate the new pitch (pitches) into students' technique.

Preparation is provided for each new skill/concept step (GETTING READY).

Basic objectives for each activity are clear (PERFORMANCE).

Supplementary activities provided for broadened experiences (ENRICHMENT). Instructors add personal teaching methods to prepare these accompaniments.

Improvisation and composition experiences are provided to encourage creative exploration of the instrument.

Music reading aids (stick notation, rhythmic syllables) are used in early pages, then transferred to standard notation.

The book's easel construction allows students to use good posture while reading the music.

INSTRUMENT GUIDE

agogo bells	conga drum	sleigh bells
bass drum	cowbell	suspended cymbal
bongo drum	finger cymbals	tambourine
brass chimes	gong	temple blocks
cabasa	guiro	triangle
claves	hand drum	vibraslap
	maracas	wood block

SG soprano glockenspiel	SM soprano metallophone	AX alto xylophone
AG alto glockenspiel	AM alto metallophone	BX bass xylophone
	BM bass metallophone	CBB contrabass bar

Joy To The World

G. F. Handel

GETTING READY

Refresh your fingers with the *D Major* scale practice patterns on page 76.

Practice the final phrase from the song carefully. Be sure to play the syncopated rhythm and the dotted rhythm accurately.

PERFORMANCE

Play the carol. Be careful not to overblow on the high notes; the pitch will go out of tune.

Sweet Betsy From Pike

American Folksong

GETTING READY

Most of *Sweet Betsy*'s rhythms are quarter notes--no problem. Slowly sight read the song. Try it again at a faster tempo.

PERFORMANCE

Play the song with guitar or piano accompaniment.

ENRICHMENT

Add this percussion ostinato to the arrangement:

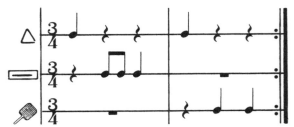

ABOUT THE RECORDER

The recorder is a whistle-type woodwind instrument belonging to the flute family, for centuries its most popular member. As early as the 12th century the recorder was used as a folk instrument. In the 16th century composers began writing for solo and ensembles of recorders made in various sizes and ranges. Elizabethan poets, playwrights and artists referred to the recorder in their works. In the Baroque period (1600-1750), the alto recorder was a popular concert instrument, admired for its sweet tone quality. Many works by Bach and Telemann feature this instrument. When larger orchestral sounds came into vogue in the late 18th century, the recorder was replaced by the transverse (side-blown) flute, the descendant of which is commonly used in bands and orchestras today.

Around 1925, a revival of interest in Renaissance and Baroque music returned the recorder to active musical life. Today recorders can be heard in TV, movie, and popular music, as well as in ensembles performing early music in churches, schools and at the professional concert level. There are six sizes, and corresponding ranges, of recorders in use today: sopranino, soprano, alto, tenor, bass, and great bass.

The soprano recorder is the one commonly used in elementary classrooms and as a recreational instrument for adults. A functional skill is relatively easy to acquire, and good plastic models are available at a modest cost. Playing the recorder, alone and with others, can provide much pleasure while introducing the player to the fundamentals of music.

HAND POSITION

The top three holes are covered by the first three fingers of the left hand; the bottom four holes are covered by the four fingers of the right hand. The left thumb covers the hole on the back of the instrument; the right thumb supports the instrument beneath the fourth and fifth holes.

Cover the holes completely with the pads of the fingers, not the fingertips. Excessive pressure is not necessary.

Arms should be slightly away from the body with shoulders relaxed.

BREATH CONTROL AND ARTICULATION

Rest the recorder's mouthpiece on your lower lip and close your mouth over it. Do not touch it with your teeth.

Breathe quickly and deeply but do not raise your shoulders.

Blow gently in a steady stream. Lowest tones require the softest blowing.

If a squeak results, it is probably because you are overblowing, or the holes are not completely covered.

Overblowing raises the pitch out of tune; underblowing lowers the pitch out of tune. Strive to play perfectly in tune.

Start the sound by articulating *duh*... as you blow gently. When you play several consecutive tones articulate them as *duh*...*duh*...*duh*....

Articulate a final ...*d* at the end of each series of tones (*duh*... *duh*...*d)* or to separate the tones completely (*duh*...*d duh*...*d*).

Tonguing, as this is called, will become automatic with practice. Exceptions to this articulation rule are explained in the text as you progress in technique.

Rund Und Rund

German Folksong

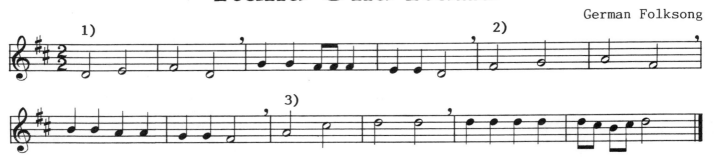

GETTING READY

Practice the final phrase of the song to gain rhythmic accuracy.

Slowly play the entire round in unison.

PERFORMANCE

Play the melody in unison.

Divide into two groups and play the melody as a two-part round.

Divide into three groups and play the melody as a three-part round.

Now Is The Month Of Maying

T. Morley

GETTING READY

Carefully practice the final phrase of the song.

Slowly sight read the entire song. Don't forget the accidentals and slurs.

PERFORMANCE

Play the song in a lively tempo.

ENRICHMENT

Improvise a hand drum part to accompany the melody.

FINGERING CHART

This fingering chart summarizes the fingerings for the pitches used in *Tutoring Tooters*. Solid circles indicate fingers covering holes; open circles indicate open holes; T indicates left thumb. Consult the complete fingering chart supplied with your recorder for fingerings not used in this book.

C D E F F# G A Bb B C C# D E

LEFT HAND

RIGHT HAND

Puer Nobis Nascitur

German Carol

GETTING READY

Sight read the song slowly.

PERFORMANCE

Play the song with a smooth flowing style.

ENRICHMENT

Add this piano accompaniment to the arrangement:

CHAPTER

BAG

Peas Porridge Hot

GETTING READY

Speak the following rhyme. As you say it, tap the **beat** at a steady, brisk **tempo**.

Peas porridge hot

Peas porridge cold

Peas porridge in the pot

Nine days old

RHYTHM TUTOR

BEAT IS THE STEADY PULSE YOU FEEL AS YOU TAP YOUR FOOT AND SAY THE VERSE.

TEMPO IS THE SPEED OF THE BEAT. TEMPOS CAN BE SLOW, MODERATE, FAST OR ANYTHING IN BETWEEN.

You probably felt the beats to the rhyme as shown below. Say the rhyme and tap the beats again; this time tap on the beat marks below:

	Peas	*por-ridge*	*hot*	
Beats:	|	|	|	|

       Peas   *por-ridge cold*
        \| \| \| \|

       Peas   *por-ridge in the pot*
        \| \| \| \|

       Nine   *days*   *old*
        \| \| \| \|

RHYTHM TUTOR

SOMETIMES THERE IS ONE SOUND PER BEAT. SOMETIMES THERE IS NO SOUND ON A BEAT. SOMETIMES THERE IS MORE THAN ONE SOUND DURING A BEAT. THE PATTERN OF SOUND AND SILENCE IS CALLED THE **RHYTHM.**

CHAPTER 10

C sharp

THE NEW PITCH

Practice each of the following patterns several times to become familiar with the new pitch and to learn how to move between pitches.

(1) (2)

(3) (4)

MELODY TUTOR

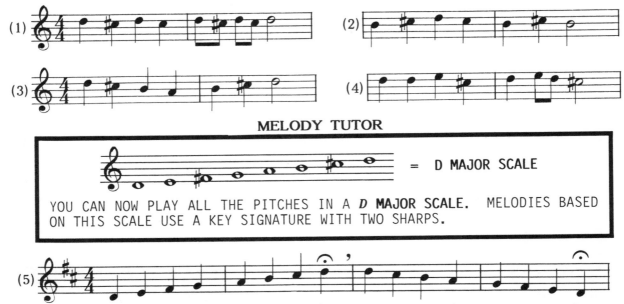

= D MAJOR SCALE

YOU CAN NOW PLAY ALL THE PITCHES IN A **D MAJOR SCALE.** MELODIES BASED ON THIS SCALE USE A KEY SIGNATURE WITH TWO SHARPS.

(5)

What famous melody (in different rhythm) does the descending *D Major* scale sound like? You'll soon find out if you can't think of it.

Old Round

German Folksong

GETTING READY

You should be able to sight read this melody. Try.

PERFORMANCE

Divide into two groups and play this melody as a two-part round.

Divide into three groups and play the melody as a three-part round.

The rhythm of the rhyme probably went like this. Say the rhyme again; tap the beats as you follow the rhythm.

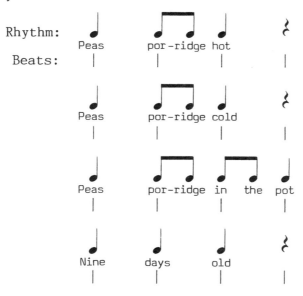

RHYTHM TUTOR

SAID ANOTHER WAY, **RHYTHM** IS THE DIVISION OF MUSICAL TIME INTO LONG OR SHORT UNITS OF SOUND OR SILENCE. WHEN WE WRITE RHYTHM ON PAPER WE USE **RHYTHMIC SYMBOLS--NOTES** AND **RESTS**.

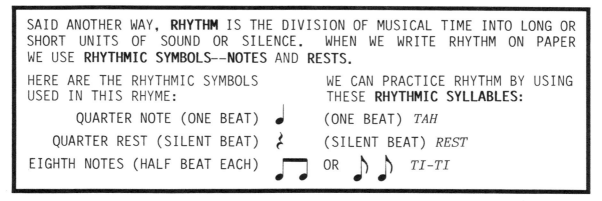

Say the rhythmic syllables for the rhyme. Read from the rhythms at the top of the page.

Play the rhyme on your recorder on the pitch *B*. Read the rhythms above.

Next, play the rhyme on *A*, then again on *G*.

Divide into two recorder groups. Half play the rhyme on *B*; half play it on *G*. Switch parts for a second playing.

TOOTER TUTOR

THINK *DUH*... AS YOU PLAY EACH NOTE. THINK *DUH*... *DUH*... *DUH*... ETC. AS YOU PLAY SEVERAL NOTES IN A ROW. BUT THINK *DUH*...*D* AS YOU PLAY THE LAST NOTE BEFORE A REST OR THE VERY LAST NOTE OF A SONG IN ORDER TO STOP THE FLOW OF AIR ACCURATELY.

Look again at the rhyme's rhythm above. How many beats did you feel in each line? What you felt was the **meter**.

Coventry Carol

Old English Carol

Lul - lay, thou lit - tle ti - ny child, bye, bye, lul -

ly, lul - lay. _____ Lul - lay, thou lit - tle

ti - ny child, bye, bye, lul - ly, lul - lay. _____

MELODY TUTOR

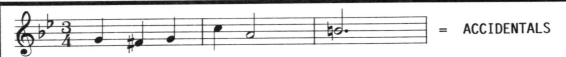 = **ACCIDENTALS**

AN **ACCIDENTAL** IS A SHARP, FLAT, OR **NATURAL** (♮) SIGN PLACED IN FRONT OF ANY NOTE.   AN ACCIDENTAL CHANGES THE KEY SIGNATURE INSTRUCTIONS FOR ONE MEASURE.   A SHARP RAISES THE PITCH OF THE NOTE A HALF STEP, A FLAT LOWERS THE PITCH OF THE NOTE A HALF STEP, AND A NATURAL CANCELS THE KEY SIGNATURE INSTRUCTION FOR ONE MEASURE.   IN THE EXAMPLE ABOVE, THE NATURAL SIGN RETURNS THE *B-FLAT* TO *B*--THE FIRST NOTE YOU LEARNED.

GETTING READY

Practice this final motive from the song containing accidentals:

Slowly play the entire song.

PERFORMANCE

Perform the carol in an A (sing) A' (recorders) form. Be sure to sustain the tied notes their full value with steady breath support.

ENRICHMENT

Add this finger cymbal part at the end of phrases 2 and 4:

PATTERNS OF RHYTHM ARE ORGANIZED INTO REPEATING SETS OF BEATS CALLED THE **METER**. THIS RHYME USES 4-BEAT SETS--**QUADRUPLE METER**.

IN WRITTEN MUSIC THE METER IS INDICATED IN TWO WAYS:
A. THE TOP NUMBER OF THE **TIME SIGNATURE** TELLS THE METER.
B. **BAR LINES** SEPARATE THE MUSIC INTO **MEASURES**. EACH MEASURE OF MUSIC CONTAINS ONE SET OF BEATS.

THE BOTTOM NUMBER IN THE TIME SIGNATURE TELLS US WHAT TYPE NOTE VALUE RECEIVES ONE BEAT--A QUARTER NOTE (OR REST) IN THIS CASE.

Peas por-ridge hot, peas por-ridge cold, peas por-ridge in the pot nine days old.

PERFORMANCE

Play the song on your recorder, reading from the music. Yes, you <u>can</u> do it!

Hot Cross Buns

Traditional

Hot cross buns, hot cross buns, one a pen-ny two a pen-ny, hot cross buns.

GETTING READY

Here is another rhyme set to music. The musical ingredients are the same as for *Peas Porridge Hot*. They are just mixed in different proportions in this recipe.

Say the rhyme in rhythm; keep a steady beat. Then say it using rhythmic syllables.

Say the rhyme in rhythm using pitch names. Rest your recorder on your chin and finger the notes as you say the pitch names.

Practice each of the following patterns from the song slowly, then faster.

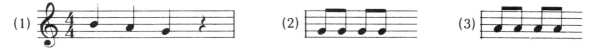

Play the entire song slowly; repeat at faster tempos.

PERFORMANCE

Play *Hot Cross Buns*.

ENRICHMENT

Add this accompaniment to the recorder melody:

Lavender's Blue

English Folksong

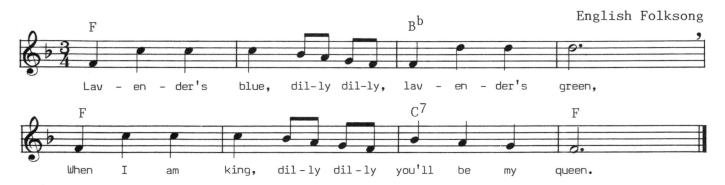

Lav - en - der's blue, dil-ly dil-ly, lav - en - der's green,

When I am king, dil-ly dil-ly you'll be my queen.

GETTING READY
Slowly sight read the song. Keep the eighth notes steady. Work on playing an entire phrase in one breath.

PERFORMANCE
Perform the song in this form: A (recorder) A' (sing) A (recorder) plus piano or guitar.

ENRICHMENT
Add the following tone color effects to the arrangement:

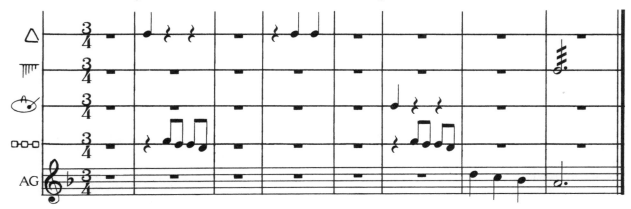

Improvisation - 4

GETTING READY
Improvise a melody using these pitches:

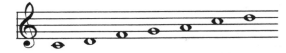

The melody should fit the following verse:

> *The Queen of Hearts she made some tarts*
> *All on a summer's day,*
> *The Knave of Hearts he stole those tarts*
> *And took them clean away.*

You may choose any meter and rhythmic motives that fit your creative ideas. Do not notate your melody--keep it in your head.

PERFORMANCE
Perform your recorder improvisation for the class.

Fais Do Do

French Folksong

Guitar/Piano

Fais do do, come let us go dream - ing, Fais do do, go dream-ing with me.

METER TUTOR

THE 3/4 TIME SIGNATURE TELLS YOU THERE WILL BE 3 BEATS PER MEASURE AND THAT A QUARTER NOTE OR REST RECEIVES ONE BEAT. THIS IS **TRIPLE METER.**

RHYTHM TUTOR

♩ = HALF NOTE

A **HALF NOTE** IS THE SAME AS TWO QUARTER NOTES COMBINED INTO ONE. WHEN A TIME SIGNATURE HAS A 4 ON THE BOTTOM A HALF NOTE IS TWO BEATS LONG. THE RHYTHMIC SYLLABLE FOR A HALF NOTE IS *TAH-AH*--ONE SOUND PER QUARTER.

GETTING READY

Practice these patterns from the song using rhythmic syllables. Keep a steady beat.

Speak the pitch names of each of the following patterns. Rest your recorder on your chin and finger the notes as you say the pitches.

Play each pattern on your recorder, slowly at first. Play the entire song--(1) (2) (1) (3).

PERFORMANCE

Play *Fais Do Do* (feh doe doe) on your recorder.

ENRICHMENT

Perform *Fais Do Do* three times: recorders, sing, recorders. Use piano or guitar.

Perform the song on recorders. Then your teacher will play the following new section. When this is over play the original melody again.

FORM TUTOR

WHEN YOU PERFORM A SONG IN DIFFERENT WAYS YOU USE DIFFERENT **FORMS.** THE FORM OF THE FIRST ENRICHMENT WAS **A A' A.** **A** IS WHATEVER COMES FIRST AND **A'** (**A PRIME**) IS REPETITION WITH A SLIGHT CHANGE. THE FINAL SECTION WAS AN EXACT REPETITION OF **A**, SO WE CALL IT **A** AGAIN.

THE FORM OF THE SECOND ENRICHMENT WAS **A B A.** THE SECOND SECTION WAS TOTALLY DIFFERENT, A CONTRAST, SO WE USE A NEW LETTER--**B.**

Good Morning To All

English Round

Good morn-ing to all, with joy let us sing, A new day is dawn-ing, let hap-pi-ness ring, Good morn - ing, good morn - ing.

GETTING READY

Note that each phrase has two motives. Slowly practice each motive, each phrase, then the entire song.

PERFORMANCE

Divide into two groups and play, then sing, the song as a two-part round.

Divide into three groups and play, then sing, the song as a three-part round.

Perform the song in this form: A (unison recorders) A' (unison voices) A'' (three-part recorder round).

Dona Nobis Pacem

Anonymous

GETTING READY

Practice the following motives from the song until you can play them smoothly:

Play the entire song slowly.

PERFORMANCE

Play the song in unison.

Divide into two groups and play the song as a two-part round.

Divide into three groups and play the song as a three-part round.

Suo Gan

Welsh Folksong

Su - o gan do not weep, Su - o gan go to sleep,

Su - o gan Moth - er's near, Su - o gan have no fear.

FORM TUTOR

A **PHRASE MARK** (,) SHOWS THE END OF A **MUSICAL PHRASE**—A MUSICAL IDEA SIMILAR TO A LINE OF A POEM OR A THOUGHT IN VERBAL COMMUNICATION. TAKE A BREATH AT EACH PHRASE MARK. TRY NOT TO BREATHE ELSEWHERE.

WHEN YOU BEGIN TO LEARN A SONG, LOOK FIRST AT ITS **PHRASE DESIGN.** YOU WILL SAVE A LOT OF PRACTICE TIME. IN THIS SONG YOU WILL DISCOVER
1. THERE ARE FOUR EQUAL-LENGTH PHRASES, EACH WITH THE SAME RHYTHM.
2. EACH PHRASE BEGINS WITH THE SAME **MOTIVE**—A SHORT, DISTINCTIVE PATTERN THAT YOU TEND TO REMEMBER.
3. PHRASES 1 AND 3 ARE EXACTLY ALIKE, AS ARE PHRASES 2 AND 4.
4. THE PHRASE DESIGN OF THE SONG IS THEREFORE **a b a b.** (LOWER CASE LETTERS DESCRIBE PHRASES; CAPITAL LETTERS DESCRIBE SECTIONS.)

GETTING READY

Speak this pattern with rhythmic syllables:

Speak the pitch names of each motive as you hold the recorder and finger the pitches.

Play each pattern on your recorder.

Slowly play the entire song.

PERFORMANCE

Perform *Suo Gan* (see-oh gahn). Use an A (sing) A' (recorders) A (sing) form.

ENRICHMENT

Perform the song as before; this time add a finger cymbal on the final beat of each phrase in the A sections.

Perform *Suo Gan* again. Your teacher will add the following harmony to the A' section.

O How Lovely Is the Evening

Traditional

O how love-ly is the eve-ning, is the eve-ning, When the bells are
sweet-ly ring-ing, sweet-ly ring-ing, Ding, dong, ding dong, ding, dong.

GETTING READY

Practice these patterns from the song. Be sure to slur where indicated.

Play the entire song slowly.

PERFORMANCE

Divide into two groups and play or sing the song as a two-part round.

Divide into three groups and play or sing the song as a three-part round.

ENRICHMENT

Add a mallet percussion instrument to each part of the round; try AM with part 1, AG with part 2, and SG with part 3. Include a piano or guitar.

Lightly Row

German Folksong

GETTING READY

Practice the following patterns from the song:

Slowly play the entire song.

PERFORMANCE

Play the song with piano or guitar accompaniment.

Trampin'

African American Spiritual

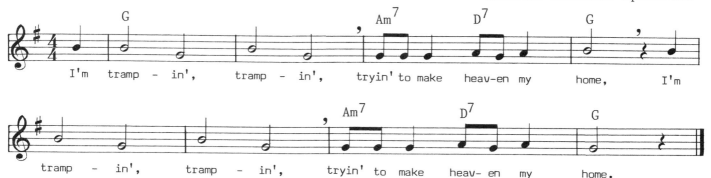

I'm tramp - in', tramp - in', tryin' to make heav-en my home, I'm

tramp - in', tramp - in', tryin' to make heav- en my home.

RHYTHM TUTOR

YOUR EXAMINATION OF THIS SONG'S PHRASE DESIGN SHOWS ANOTHER **a b a b** DESIGN BUT THE FIRST AND THIRD PHRASES BEGIN WITH AN EXTRA **PICK-UP BEAT;** THE PHRASE BEGINS ONE BEAT BEFORE THE FIRST MEASURE. PICK-UP BEATS MAKE THE **DOWNBEAT** (BEAT 1 OF THE NEXT MEASURE) FEEL STRONGER. YOU SHOULD HAVE NO TROUBLE FIGURING OUT WHY THE UNKNOWN COMPOSER OF THIS SPIRITUAL WANTED THIS EFFECT.

WHEN A SONG BEGINS WITH A PICK-UP BEAT, THE FINAL MEASURE WILL BE A BEAT SHORT IN ORDER TO KEEP THE CORRECT NUMBER OF BEATS PER MEASURE.

GETTING READY

Speak these patterns with rhythmic syllables:

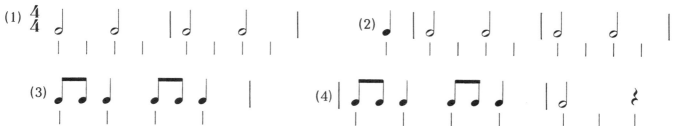

Speak the pitch names of these patterns as you finger the notes on your recorder:

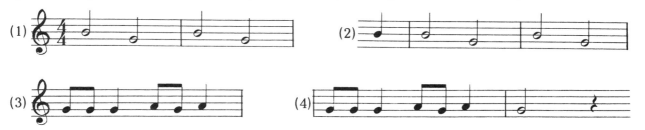

Play each pattern on your recorder; begin slowly and keep the beat steady.

Slowly play the entire song. Play it again at a livelier tempo.

PERFORMANCE

Perform *Trampin'* with an A A' A form of your choice. Include piano or guitar accompaniment if you wish.

New River Train

American Folksong

Rid-in' on that new riv-er train, _____ Rid-in' on that
new riv-er train, _____ Same old train that brought me
here, Goin' to car-ry me back a - gain. _____

GETTING READY

Practice these interval patterns from the song:

Practice the entire song slowly. Give full rhythm value to the tied notes.

PERFORMANCE

Perform the song in this form: A (sing) A' (recorder) A" (both). Add piano or guitar if desired.

ENRICHMENT

Add train sounds to the arrangement, such as cabasa playing quarter notes for the first half, then eighth notes for the second half, plus recorders playing this chord during all tied notes. The curved line trailing from the half note calls for a **falloff.** Let your air support drop near the end of the note to simulate a steam engine whistle. NOTE: This is the only time in the entire book when you are <u>supposed</u> to sound like this!

Sleep Baby Sleep

German Folksong

Sleep ba-by sleep,   sleep ba-by sleep.   Moth-er shakes the dream-land tree and

from it falls a dream for thee,   sleep   ba - by sleep.

MELODY TUTOR

FROM NOW ON WE WILL USUALLY COMBINE RHYTHM AND MELODY PRACTICES. YOU
CAN CONTINUE TO DO THE SEPARATE PRACTICES (SYLLABLES, SPOKEN PITCHES,
PLAYED PITCHES) AS LONG AS THEY HELP YOU, BUT TRY TO COMBINE RHYTHMIC
SYLLABLES WITH SPOKEN PITCHES. THEN COMBINE EVERYTHING INTO A SINGLE
PRACTICE, ESPECIALLY IF NEW MOTIVES ARE NOT TOO DIFFICULT.

GETTING READY

Practice the following motives from the song. Begin with rhythmic syllables only if you
are unsure of the rhythm. Speak the pitch names of the motives as you finger the notes on
your recorder:

(1)    (2)

PERFORMANCE

Perform the song. Use an A A' A" form of your choice (recorder, sing, recorder and
sing, in any order). Perform each phrase in a **legato** (smoothly connected) style.

FORM TUTOR

A" MEANS **A DOUBLE PRIME**. IF **A** IS THE FIRST MAIN SECTION AND **A'** IS A
REPETITION OF THIS SECTION WITH A SMALL CHANGE, THEN **A"** IS ANOTHER
REPETITION OF THE SECTION WITH A DIFFERENT SMALL CHANGE.

ENRICHMENT

Perform the song with this accompaniment:

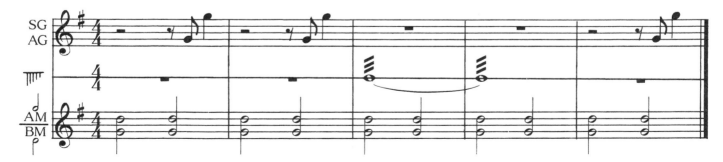

CHAPTER 6

B flat

THE NEW PITCH

Practice each of the following patterns several times to become familiar with the new pitch and to learn how to move between pitches.

MELODY TUTOR

♭ = FLAT

WHEN A **FLAT** IS PLACED IN FRONT OF A NOTE, THE PITCH OF THAT NOTE IS LOWERED BY A HALF STEP--TO THE NEXT POSSIBLE LOWER PITCH. ALL REPETITIONS OF THE SAME NOTE IN THE SAME MEASURE ARE ALSO CHANGED.

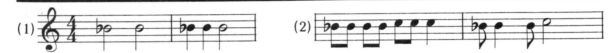

MELODY TUTOR

= B-FLAT IN THE KEY SIGNATURE

WHEN THERE IS A FLAT ON THE *B* LINE IN THE KEY SIGNATURE, ALL *B*s IN THE COMPOSITION ARE CHANGED TO *B-FLATS*.

In these practice patterns the *B-flat* symbol has been moved to the key signature. All *B*s are now changed to *B-flats*.

Establish a tempo and keep it steady throughout. Can you play every measure?

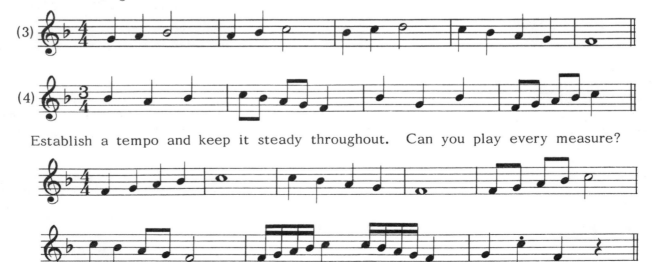

70

Babylon's Falling

African American Spiritual

Bab- y-lon's fall-ing, fall- ing, fall-ing, Bab- y-lon's fall-ing to rise no more.

METER TUTOR

THE $\frac{2}{4}$ TIME SIGNATURE TELLS YOU THERE WILL BE 2 BEATS PER MEASURE AND THAT A QUARTER NOTE OR REST RECEIVES ONE BEAT. THIS IS **DUPLE METER.**

RHYTHM TUTOR

♪ = SIXTEENTH NOTE   = SIXTEENTH NOTES

A **SIXTEENTH NOTE** EQUALS $\frac{1}{4}$ OF A QUARTER NOTE. WHEN A TIME SIGNATURE HAS A 4 ON THE BOTTOM THERE ARE FOUR SIXTEENTH NOTES PER BEAT.

FORM TUTOR

= DOUBLE BAR   = REPEAT SIGN

A **DOUBLE BAR** WITH ONE THIN AND ONE THICK LINE INDICATES THE END OF A COMPOSITION. BUT WHEN DOTS ARE PLACED ABOVE AND BELOW THE MIDDLE STAFF LINE, A **REPEAT SIGN** IS FORMED. REPEAT THE ENTIRE SECTION.

GETTING READY

Practice these motives from the song as needed. Begin slowly; tongue precisely.

Rhythmic syllables: ti-ri ti   ti   ti   ti-ri ti   ti   ti-ri

PERFORMANCE

Perform the song softly using this form: A (recorder) A' (sing) A" (recorder and sing). Repeat the three-section sequence two more times, each a little faster. Add piano or guitar accompaniment if you wish.

ENRICHMENT

Perform the song in an A B A form. For the B section remove all *C* and *F* bars from several xylophones. Xylophone players will play any pitches in the rhythm of the song for the B section. This is called **melodic improvisation.**

Hallelu

Trinidad Folksong

Sing to the mu - sic, hal - le - lu. _   Sing to the mu - sic, hal - le - lu. _
La la la la la la la la. _   La la la la la la la la. _

Sing to the mu - sic, hal - le - lu. _   Sing to the mu - sic, hal - le - lu. _
La la la la la, la la la. _   La la la la la la la la. _

GETTING READY

Clap each of these rhythms--the first phrase of the harmony and the melody:

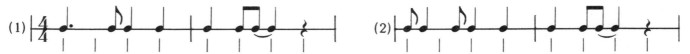

Divide into two groups and clap the rhythms at the same time. Switch parts.

Sight sing the melody. Two or three recorders can play along to help.

All recorders practice the harmony line. Divide into two groups--half play this harmony line, half sing the melody.

PERFORMANCE

Perform the song this this form: A (sing melody) A' (sing melody with recorder harmony) A" (recorders play melody and harmony). A guitar accompaniment is also suggested.

ENRICHMENT

Add the following accompaniment. In addition bongos can improvise on the repeat. Keep the guitar accompaniment.

Improvisation - 1

A

FORM TUTOR

QUESTION AND ANSWER PHRASES IN MUSIC ARE SHORT PAIRS OF PHRASES THAT TOGETHER FORM A COMPLETE MUSICAL IDEA. THE QUESTION, THE OPENING PHRASE, BEGINS THE IDEA BUT LEAVES IT UNFINISHED. THE ANSWER PHRASE REPEATS SOME OF THE RHYTHMIC AND MELODIC MATERIAL IN THE QUESTION BUT ALWAYS ENDS WITH A MORE FINAL FEELING. *FAIS DO DO* (p. 4) AND *SUO GAN* (p. 5) ARE GOOD EXAMPLES OF SIMPLE QUESTION/ANSWER PHRASE MELODIES.

PERFORMANCE

(1) It is time to **improvise** melodies on your recorder. Your teacher will play the first phrase of melody A--the question. Following this, play an answer phrase using *B*, *A*, or *G*. You may use the same rhythm as the question and repeat the opening melodic motive in your answer, but be sure to create a different conclusion.

(2) This time vary more of the question's rhythm in your answer. Two or three of you may be asked to play the question in place of your teacher.

(3) Now you will asked to play your answer as part of a duet or trio, that is, two or three at a time. You will each play your own improvisation. If you feel brave, volunteer for a solo answer.

(4) Make up a new improvised answer. Be sure that some of your rhythms and pitches are different from those of the question.

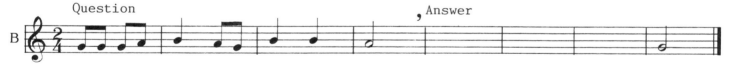

B

Repeat the above five improvisation steps with melody B.

C

Repeat the five improvisation steps with melody C.

All Through The Night

Welsh Folksong

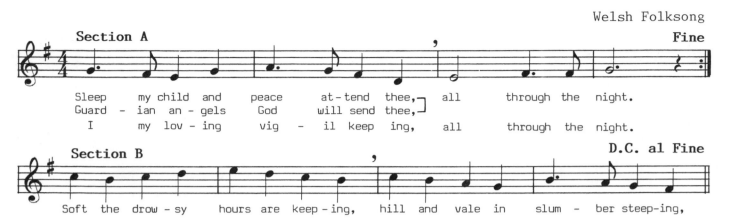

Section A

Sleep   my child and   peace at-tend thee,   all   through the night.
Guard - ian an - gels   God   will send thee,   all   through the night.
I   my lov - ing   vig - il keep ing,   all   through the night.

Section B

Soft   the drow - sy   hours are keep - ing,   hill and vale in   slum - ber steep-ing,

GETTING READY

Practice the song slowly, noting the roadsigns. If you sing the song, the third line of lyrics in section A is sung only on the D.C.

Does this song seem easy to learn? It should, because you have already played section A in chapter 4--page 37.

PERFORMANCE

Perform the song as written, either on recorders or sung.

ENRICHMENT

Add the following piano accompaniment to the song:

68

The Cricket's Lullaby

Traditional

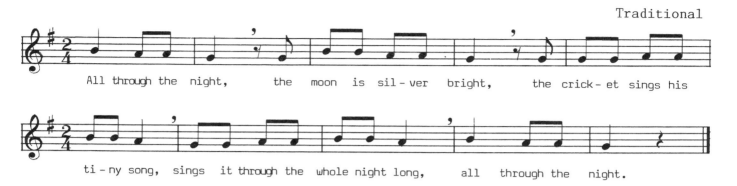

All through the night, the moon is sil-ver bright, the crick-et sings his

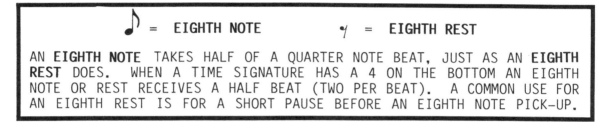

ti-ny song, sings it through the whole night long, all through the night.

RHYTHM TUTOR

♪ = EIGHTH NOTE   𝄾 = EIGHTH REST

AN **EIGHTH NOTE** TAKES HALF OF A QUARTER NOTE BEAT, JUST AS AN **EIGHTH REST** DOES. WHEN A TIME SIGNATURE HAS A 4 ON THE BOTTOM AN EIGHTH NOTE OR REST RECEIVES A HALF BEAT (TWO PER BEAT). A COMMON USE FOR AN EIGHTH REST IS FOR A SHORT PAUSE BEFORE AN EIGHTH NOTE PICK-UP.

GETTING READY
Practice these patterns:

Play the entire song, slowly.

PERFORMANCE
Perform the song in a form of your choice.

ENRICHMENT
Play the song again. Your teacher will add this harmony part as you play the melody.

What's Little Babies Made Of?

Appalachian Folksong

What's lit-tle ba-bies made of, made of? What's lit-tle ba-bies made of? _____

Sug-ar and crumbs and all sweet things. That's what lit-tle ba-bies made of.

GETTING READY

Listen to your teacher play melody 1 on recorder. Note the slow, rocking feeling created by the compound meter. Sing the song as your teacher it again.

Practice this motive from the song:

Play the entire song slowly.

Practice melody 2. Do you recognize it as a childhood taunting chant?

PERFORMANCE

Sing melody 1 as a solo recorder plays melody 2.

Play melody 1 on recorder as a solo SG plays melody 2.

ENRICHMENT

Add the following accompaniment and perform the song in this form: A (sing melody 1) A' (sing melody 1, recorders play melody 2) A" (recorders play melody 1, SG plays melody 2). The following percussion play throughout:

Bow Wow Wow

Bow wow wow, whose dog art thou? Lit-tle Tom-my Tink-er's dog, bow wow wow.

GETTING READY

Say this nursery rhyme in rhythm.

Composing a melody for a specific rhythm is similar to improvising answer phrases as you did in *Improvisation-1*. But now you will write down your musical ideas using standard notation. The following steps are suggestions to get you started. If you have a flair for composing, you will develop your own method soon enough.

Using *B*, *A*, and *G*, try out different pitches on your recorder for measure 1. When you have something you like, pencil in the pitches.

As you try different pitches for measure 2, be sure to play measure 1 first so that it sounds like a continuous melody.

Repeat this process for measures 3 and 4. Always play what you have already written. Your melody will sound more "finished" if you end it on G.

PERFORMANCE

Take turns with others and perform your song.

ENRICHMENT

Ask a neighbor to perform your song from your manuscript. You add some percussion improvisation (special effects, ostinato, etc.).

Maybe you had a hard time deciding what to write because you had numerous ideas that all seemed good. Here's your chance to write *Bow Wow **Wow!***

All Night, All Day

African American Spiritual

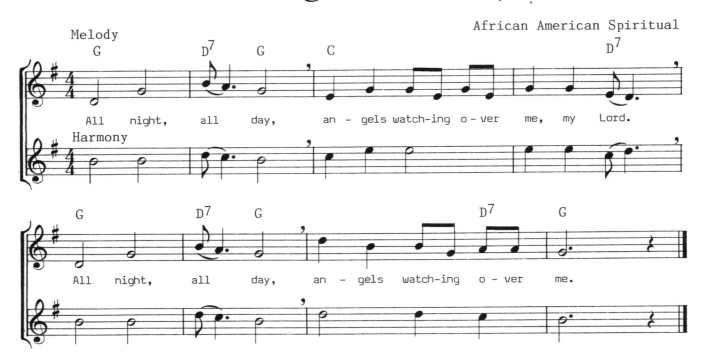

All night, all day, an-gels watch-ing o-ver me, my Lord.

All night, all day, an-gels watch-ing o-ver me.

GETTING READY

Practice the slurred notes from the song:

Play the entire song slowly; first the melody, then the harmony.

PERFORMANCE

Perform the song in this form: A (recorder, melody only) A' (sing melody) A" (recorder, melody and harmony). Also add piano or guitar.

Ridin' In The Buggy

Western Play Party

Rid-in' in the bug-gy, Miss Ma-ry Jane, Miss Ma-ry Jane, Miss Ma-ry Jane,

Rid-in' in the bug-gy, Miss Ma-ry Jane, I'm a long way from home.

RHYTHM TUTOR

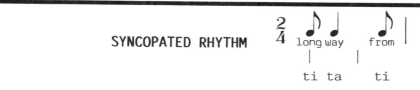

SYNCOPATED RHYTHM

THIS IS A TYPE OF **SYNCOPATED RHYTHM**--AN OFF-BEAT RHYTHM. *WAY* BEGINS IN BETWEEN BEATS, OFF THE BEAT, AND IS SUSTAINED THROUGH THE BEGIN-NING OF THE NEXT BEAT. SYNCOPATED RHYTHMS ADD A LITTLE PUSH, OR LEAN, TO THE FORWARD MOTION OF THE MUSIC.

GETTING READY
Speak the words in rhythm as you tap a steady beat.

Practice these patterns from the song, slowly, then more rapidly:

Play the entire song slowly.

PERFORMANCE
Play the song in as brisk a tempo as possible. Play each line as one phrase if you can. Perform the song in an A A' A form. Include piano or guitar accompaniment if you want to.

ENRICHMENT
Add sleigh bells (for winter) or temple blocks (for spring) in a steady eighth note rhythm.

America

H. Cary

TOOTER TUTOR

SLURS LOOK LIKE TIES, BUT SLURS CONNECT TWO OR MORE <u>DIFFERENT</u> NOTES IN A SPECIAL WAY. ARTICULATE THE FIRST NOTE UNDER OR OVER A SLUR IN THE USUAL WAY (*DUH*...). DO NOT TONGUE ANY FOLLOWING NOTES UNDER THE SLUR. LET THE CHANGE OF FINGERING TAKE THE PLACE OF THE TONGUED ARTICULATION. SLURRED NOTES SIMULATE THE WAY WE SING ON A SINGLE SYLLABLE TWO OR MORE DIFFERENT PITCHES.

GETTING READY

Slowly practice the following patterns:

Slowly practice the final two phrases of the song.

Play the entire song slowly.

PERFORMANCE

Play the song.

Who's That Yonder?

African American Spiritual

Who's that yon–der dressed in red? Must be the child–ren that Mo–ses led.

Who's that yon–der dressed in white? Must be the child–ren of the Is–rael – ite.

RHYTHM TUTOR

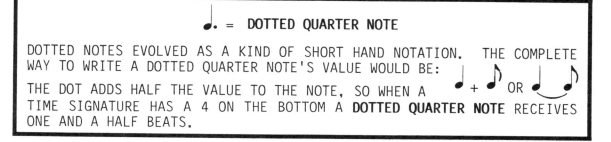

♩. = DOTTED QUARTER NOTE

DOTTED NOTES EVOLVED AS A KIND OF SHORT HAND NOTATION. THE COMPLETE WAY TO WRITE A DOTTED QUARTER NOTE'S VALUE WOULD BE: ♩ + ♪ OR ♩ ♪

THE DOT ADDS HALF THE VALUE TO THE NOTE, SO WHEN A TIME SIGNATURE HAS A 4 ON THE BOTTOM A **DOTTED QUARTER NOTE** RECEIVES ONE AND A HALF BEATS.

GETTING READY

Practice these motives from the song. HINT: When moving between *B* and *G*, lift or place both fingers down at the same time.

Motive 1 contains another type of syncopated rhythm. The second note begins in between beats and is sustained through the next beat. Be sure to place the second note exactly in the middle of beats 1 and 2.

PERFORMANCE

Perform the song with an A A' A form of your choice.

Divide into two groups. Half play phrases 1 and 3 (the question); half play phrases 2 and 4 (the answer). Trade parts.

ENRICHMENT

Add this **ostinato** (repeating pattern) as you sing or play the song:

BX

Pretty Little Girl

Tennessee Folksong

GETTING READY

Slowly practice each phrase of the song. Say the lyrics first to help you keep the rhythm patterns in mind.

PERFORMANCE

Perform the song in this form: A (sing verse 1) A' (recorder) A (sing verse 2) A' (recorders). The second verse is:

> *Bright blue eyes and curly hair* (3 times), *See me cross the water.*

NOTE: The rhythm for verse 2 is:

ENRICHMENT

Add this percussion accompaniment to the song:

Standin' In The Need Of Prayer

African American Spiritual

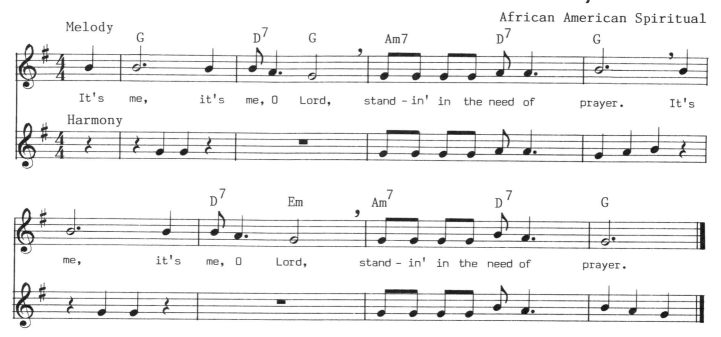

Melody

It's me, it's me, O Lord, stand - in' in the need of prayer. It's

Harmony

me, it's me, O Lord, stand - in' in the need of prayer.

RHYTHM TUTOR

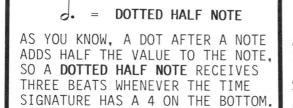

𝅗𝅥. = DOTTED HALF NOTE

AS YOU KNOW, A DOT AFTER A NOTE ADDS HALF THE VALUE TO THE NOTE, SO A **DOTTED HALF NOTE** RECEIVES THREE BEATS WHENEVER THE TIME SIGNATURE HAS A 4 ON THE BOTTOM.

▬ = WHOLE REST

A **WHOLE REST** RECEIVES FOUR BEATS OF SILENCE IN 4/4 TIME--A WHOLE MEASURE.

A SECONDARY USE FOR A WHOLE REST IS TO REPRESENT A WHOLE MEASURE OF REST REGARDLESS OF THE METER.

GETTING READY

Practice the following motives from the song. Be sure to hold the dotted half notes for three full beats and the syncopated dotted quarter notes for one and a half beats.

Play the entire melody, slowly.

Practice the harmony part. Be sure to count four beats of silence for the whole rest.

Divide into two groups and play melody and harmony together, slowly.

PERFORMANCE

Perform the melody only in an A A' A form.
Include piano or guitar accompaniment.

Divide into two groups and play the melody and harmony together, slowly.

ENRICHMENT

Add these percussion ostinatos to the arrangement:

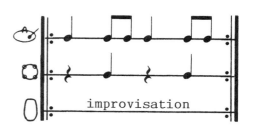

improvisation

14

Music Alone Shall Live

Traditional

GETTING READY

Practice this opening motive from the song:

This rhythmic motive occurs four times with varying pitches. Locate each motive and practice it.

Play the entire song slowly.

PERFORMANCE

Everyone play the song in unison.

Divide into two groups and play the song as a two-part round.

Divide into three groups and play the song as a three-part round.

Frère Jacques

French Folksong

GETTING READY

Everyone knows how this famous round goes, but practice the third phrase slowly at first to make sure your tongue-finger coordination is accurate.

Play the entire song slowly.

PERFORMANCE

Divide into two groups and play the song as a two-part round.

Divide into three groups and play the song as a three-part round.

Divide into four groups and play the song as a four-part round.

ENRICHMENT

Add this ostinato accompaniment to the arrangement:

The Boatman

African American Folksong

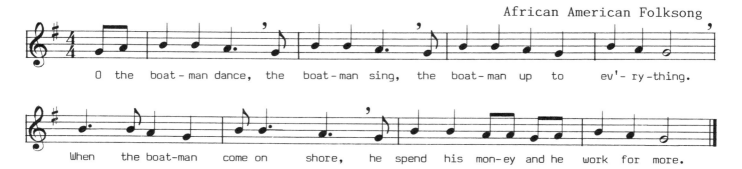

O the boat-man dance, the boat-man sing, the boat-man up to ev'-ry-thing.

When the boat-man come on shore, he spend his mon-ey and he work for more.

GETTING READY

Boatman uses only B, A, and G, like the other songs in this chapter, but this finale will seem more complex because it uses a different rhythm motive in each of its five phrases. Check this out. Read from the music above and practice one phrase at a time. Begin by saying the lyrics in rhythm; then play each phrase on your recorder. After you learn each phrase, add it to the previously learned phrases so you build your ability to play the entire song.

PERFORMANCE

Perform the song with an A A' form.

ENRICHMENT

Add the following accompaniment to the song:

CHAPTER 8

THE NEW PITCH

Practice each of the following patterns several times to become familiar with the new pitch and to learn how to move between this and the other pitches you know.

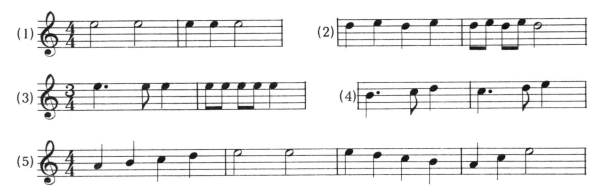

Auld Lang Syne

Scottish Air

GETTING READY

Practice the song's opening motive:

This rhythmic motive occurs six times in the song, each with different pitches. Locate each motive and practice it.

Play the entire song slowly.

PERFORMANCE

Play the song with smoothly connected pitches.

CHAPTER 2

T   E

THE NEW PITCH

Play each pattern several times to become familiar with the new pitch and to learn how to move between pitches. HINT: *E* requires slightly less air pressure than *B*, *A*, or *G*.

Bye Baby Bunting

Traditional

Bye   ba - by bunt - ing,   Dad - dy's gone a - hunt - ing,

Gone to get a rab - bit skin to wrap a ba - by bunt - ing in.

GETTING READY

Practice the following patterns. Your examination of the song's phrase design shows you that each phrase uses exactly the same pitch sequence, but with slightly different rhythms each time. When you can play the two patterns below you can play the song.

Slowly play the entire song.

PERFORMANCE

Perform the song with an A (recorders) A' (sing) form.

ENRICHMENT

Add this ostinato to the arrangement:

Hanukkah

Hebrew Folksong

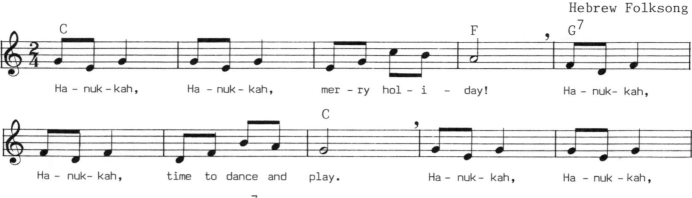

Ha - nuk - kah, Ha - nuk - kah, mer - ry hol - i - day! Ha - nuk- kah,

Ha - nuk- kah, time to dance and play. Ha - nuk - kah, Ha - nuk -kah,

bright the can -dles burn. Round and round, round and round, watch the drey- dl turn.

GETTING READY

Practice these interval patterns taken from the song--slowly then faster.

Sight read the song. Keep a steady tempo.

PERFORMANCE

Perform the song in this form: A (sing) A' (recorder) A" (both). Add piano or guitar to the accompaniment.

ENRICHMENT

Bring a dreydl to class and spin it during the last phrase of the song.

Add this tambourine part to the accompaniment:

Add a dance using the grape- vine step.

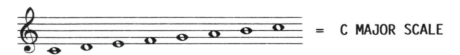

MELODY TUTOR

= C MAJOR SCALE

THE *C MAJOR SCALE* USES THE SEVEN DIFFERENT PITCHES OF THE WHITE KEYS ON A PIANO. (THE *C* IS REPEATED IN THE EXAMPLE.) MAJOR SCALES, LIKE PENTATONIC ONES, HAVE A TONIC PITCH--A HOME TONE. THE TONIC PITCH OF THIS SCALE IS *C*.

ALL THE TONES IN THE SCALE DO NOT HAVE TO BE USED IN A MELODY WRITTEN IN THE **KEY** OF *C* MAJOR, BUT IN *HANUKKAH* ALL SEVEN ARE PRESENT.

Hosisipa

Native American Folksong

Ho - si - si - pa, ho - si - si - pa, ho - si - si - pa ho - si!

GETTING READY

Chant the text several times.

Say pitch names in rhythm while you finger the pitches on your recorder. Note that the pitches usually change <u>after</u> the downbeat.

Play the entire song slowly, then a little faster.

PERFORMANCE

Perform the chant in this form: A (sing) A' (recorder) A" (sing with recorder).

ENRICHMENT

Eight to ten sit in a circle, each with a small rock in front. Play the rock passing game (see below) as you chant. (Another group plays recorders.) Increase the tempo with each repetition. Add the percussion ostinato for even more fun.

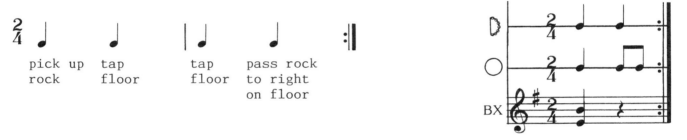

pick up   tap   tap   pass rock
rock   floor   floor   to right
                                on floor

Rocky Mountain

Section A

Rock - y Moun-tain, Rock - y Moun-tain, Rock - y Moun-tain high, When you're on that

Rock - y Moun-tain hang your head and cry.

Section B

Do, do, do, do, do re-mem-ber me. Do, do, do, do, do re-mem-ber me.

GETTING READY

Practice these patterns, slowly then faster:

Practice the entire song--not too fast.

PERFORMANCE

Play the song once, then sing it once. Add piano or guitar.

Good News

African American Spiritual

Good news, Char - iot's com - ing, good news, Char - iot's com - ing,

Good news, Char - iot's com - ing, don't want it leav-in' me be - hind.

GETTING READY

When you can play this motive you'll be ready to play the song! Go slowly at first.

PERFORMANCE

Perform the song with an A (sing) A' (recorders) form. Add piano or guitar.

ENRICHMENT

Add this tambourine part:

60

Boat Song

Chinese Folksong

MELODY TUTOR

THE SHAPE THE MELODY MAKES AS IT MOVES UP AND DOWN ON THE STAFF IS CALLED ITS **MELODIC CONTOUR**. FREQUENTLY THE MELODIC CONTOUR SUGGESTS AN ACTION IN THE MUSIC. IN THIS CASE THE SMOOTH UP AND DOWN MOTION OF THE FIRST PHRASE, REPEATED TWO MORE TIMES, SUGGESTS THE ACTION OF THE BOAT MOVING GENTLY UP AND DOWN IN THE OCEAN SWELLS.

GETTING READY

Sight read the melody at a slow tempo with smooth articulation.

PERFORMANCE

Play the song at a relaxed tempo.

ENRICHMENT

Perform the song with accompaniment shown below. The AX should improvise **glissandos** (smoothly brushing the mallet back and forth over the bars) to suggest ocean waves.

Your teacher will play this alto recorder harmony line as you play the song in this form:
A (soprano recorder melody plus all instruments except temple blocks),
A' (soprano recorder melody, alto recorder harmony plus same instruments as A),
A" (soprano recorder melody, alto recorder harmony plus all instruments).

Mary Had a Baby

African American Spiritual

Ma-ry had a ba - by, my Lord. Ma-ry had a ba - by, yes, my Lord.

Ma-ry had a ba - by, my Lord, The peo-ple keep a-com-in' but the train done gone.

GETTING READY

Slowly practice these patterns:

(1)    (2)

Slowly sight read the song.

PERFORMANCE

Perform the song with an A (sing) A' (recorders) form.

Divide into three vocal or recorder groups. Each group sings/plays one phrase, then all join together for the final phrase.

ENRICHMENT

Add this accompaniment to the arrangement:

White Sand and Gray Sand

Traditional

White sand and gray sand, Who'll buy my white sand, Who'll buy my gray sand?

GETTING READY

Everyone practice the melody. NOTE: two beats per measure, half note gets one beat.

PERFORMANCE

Divide into two groups and perform the song as a two-part round. Play it all twice.

Divide into three groups and perform the song as a three-part round. Play it all twice.

Add a solo voice to each part and perform the three-part round again.

Giddy Up, My Burro

New Mexico Folksong

Gid - dy up my bur - ro, we're go - ing to Be - lén, Fi-
es - ta is to - mor - row and one next day a - gain.

GETTING READY

There are no new melodic or rhythmic patterns in this song, so why not try to sight read the song at a slow tempo?

PERFORMANCE

Perform the song with an A A' A form.

ENRICHMENT

Add this accompaniment to the arrangement:

Who Has Seen The Wind?

Carol King*

GETTING READY

Practice each of the following patterns slowly. Then find the motive in the song that is derived from each pattern and slowly play the motives.

PERFORMANCE

Play the melody with guitar or piano accompaniment. You may also enjoy this melody as a two-part canon.

ENRICHMENT

Add an improvised chime bar part to the arrangement.

*Used by permission.
Based on a text by
Christina Rossetti.

Viva La Musica

M. Praetorius

Vi - va, vi - va la mu - si - ca. Vi - va, vi - va la

mu - si - ca. Vi - va _____ la mu - si - ca.

GETTING READY

Practice this final phrase from the song. Remember, a tie combines the rhythm values of the two notes into one longer note.

Everyone practice the song in unison.

PERFORMANCE

Perform the song in an A (sing in unison) A' (recorders in unison) form.

Divide into two recorder groups and perform the song as a two-part round.

Divide into three groups and perform the song as a three-part round.

Old Texas - Canon

American Folksong

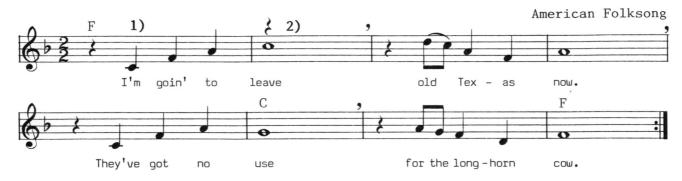

I'm goin' to leave old Tex - as now.

They've got no use for the long - horn cow.

GETTING READY

Practice the following patterns.

Practice the song slowly, four beats per measure. When you can play it fast enough, feel the music two beats per measure. Be sure to sustain the whole note a full measure.

Practice the song slowly again as a two-part canon. NOTE: The second part begins when part 1 gets to the second beat of the second measure.

PERFORMANCE

Divide into two groups and perform the song with an A (sing in canon) A' (play in canon) form. Add piano or guitar if you wish.

Jack Be Nimble

GETTING READY

Speak this rhyme; keep a steady beat. Place beat lines under the syllables where you feel the beats.

Jack be nim - ble

Beats:

Jack be quick

Jack jump o - ver the

Can - dle - stick

Say the rhyme again. Note the uneven feeling to most of the rhythm.

Say the verse again and follow the rhythm used in the song below.

Traditional

Jack   be nim - ble, Jack   be quick,   Jack   jump o - ver the can - dle-stick.

You felt two beats in each line of the verse (each measure of the music too), so why does the time signature say there are 6 beats in each measure ($\frac{6}{8}$)?

METER TUTOR

$\frac{6}{8}$ IS A **COMPOUND METER**

IN **COMPOUND METERS** THREE BEATS CAN BE COMPOUNDED (COMBINED) INTO ONE WHEN THE TEMPO IS BRISK. SO, RATHER THAN FEELING ALL SIX BEATS IN EACH MEASURE OF *JACK*, YOU FELT JUST TWO. EACH COMPOUND BEAT HAS A VALUE OF THREE EIGHTHS IN THIS SONG. THE FOLLOWING RHYTHM PATTERNS CAN ALL BE FELT AS ONE COMPOUND BEAT:

Practice the following rhythm patterns on *G*, *A*, or *E*. Think of the rhyme's rhythm as you practice.

Play phrase 1 of the song several times on your recorder.

Play phrase 2 several times.

PERFORMANCE

Perform the song. Use an A A' A form.

Woodchuck Tooter Twister

GETTING READY

All together, say the familiar woodchuck tongue twister.

How much wood would a woodchuck chuck if a woodchuck could chuck wood?

Remember the rhythm of the verse as you practice each line of the tooter twister on recorder. Be careful not to overblow and get a higher pitch than you intend.

PERFORMANCE

Divide into three groups and play the twister three times, as follows:
first time, part 1 only; second time, parts 1 and 2; third time, all three parts.

Change parts and play it again. You could also reverse the order of entrances.

Scarborough Fair

English Folksong

Are you go-ing to Scar-bo-rough fair? Pars-ley, sage, rose-ma-ry and thyme. Re-

mem-ber me to one who lives there. She was once a true love of mine.

GETTING READY

Practice this motive from the song. Be sure to play the dotted rhythms accurately.

Slowly sight read the song. Play each phrase smoothly.

PERFORMANCE

Perform the song with an A (sing) A' (recorders) form.

Witches' Dance

S. McRae

METER TUTOR

REMINDER: AT A BRISK TEMPO IN THIS COMPOUND METER:

A DOTTED QUARTER NOTE (♩.) = ONE BEAT;

A DOTTED HALF NOTE (𝅗𝅥.) = TWO BEATS.

GETTING READY

Play these rhythms on *G*, *A*, or *E*.

Practice each phrase of the melody slowly.

PERFORMANCE

Perform the song several times, each time faster.

ENRICHMENT

Perform the tune with the following accompaniment:

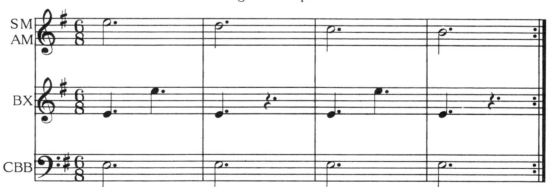

Make up a spooky rhyme to use as a new A section. (The song will become section B.) Here is a sample:

> *Olliga bolliga boo,*
> *The witches are stirring their brew,*
> *Ickery dickery doon,*
> *They dance by the light of the moon.*

Perform *Witches' Dance* in this form: A (spooky rhyme) B (recorder melody with accompaniment instruments) A' (sticks or drums play the rhythm of the rhyme) B (as before; add a single gong stroke at the end). Guaranteed spooky.

21

CHAPTER 7

THE NEW PITCHES

Practice each of the following patterns several times to become familiar with the new pitches and to learn how to move between these and the other pitches you know. Be sure to cover the holes securely. NOTE: Low *C* requires very gentle air flow.

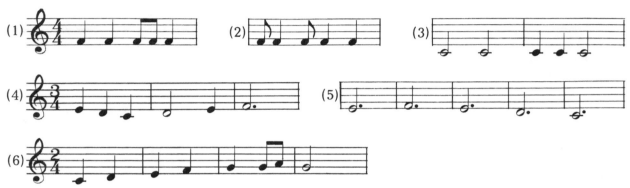

Coral

American Folksong

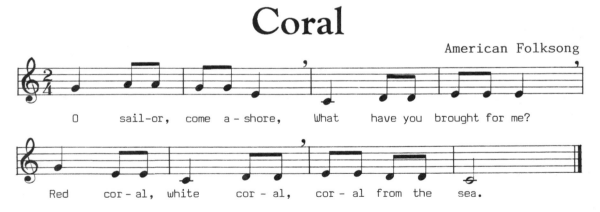

O   sail-or,   come a-shore,   What   have you brought for me?

Red   cor-al, white   cor-al,   cor-al from the   sea.

GETTING READY

Practice this pattern to achieve a smooth, even tone:

Play the entire song slowly to achieve the same even flow of sound.

PERFORMANCE

Perform the song in this form: A (recorder) A' (sing) A" (both).

The Train's Off The Track

Virginia Folksong

O, the train's off the track and I can't get it back, and I can't get a let-ter to my home. To my home, to my home, and I can't get a let-ter to my home.

RHYTHM TUTOR

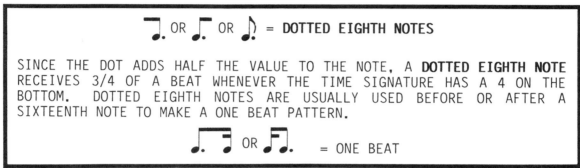

♪. OR ♪. OR ♪ = DOTTED EIGHTH NOTES

SINCE THE DOT ADDS HALF THE VALUE TO THE NOTE, A **DOTTED EIGHTH NOTE** RECEIVES 3/4 OF A BEAT WHENEVER THE TIME SIGNATURE HAS A 4 ON THE BOTTOM. DOTTED EIGHTH NOTES ARE USUALLY USED BEFORE OR AFTER A SIXTEENTH NOTE TO MAKE A ONE BEAT PATTERN.

♪. ♪ OR ♪♪. = ONE BEAT

GETTING READY

Practice the following motives. The interval patterns of examples 4-6 are taken from the song. Be sure to play the sixteenth note in pattern 6 very quickly; it is only $\frac{1}{4}$ beat long. Some call this rhythm of a sixteenth followed by a dotted eighth note a **Scottish snap** because it is often found in the folk music of Scotland.

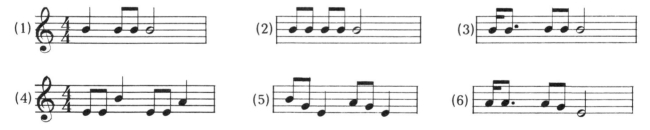

PERFORMANCE

Perform the song with a A A' A form, with or without piano or guitar.

ENRICHMENT

Add a triangle | ξ ♪♪ ♩ | in every measure that begins with *home*.

Go Tell Aunt Rhody - Trio

GETTING READY
Practice this pattern.

Slowly sight read the song; first the melody, then harmony 1, then harmony 2.

PERFORMANCE
Play the melody with piano or guitar accompaniment.

Divide into three recorder groups and play the song in this form: A (melody) A' (melody and harmony 1) A" (all three parts). Exchange parts and perform again.

Jelly In The Bowl

GETTING READY
Speak the rhyme in quadruple meter; then notate your rhythm on the line above the words.

Write a melody for your rhythm. Use pitches from the *G pentatonic* scale shown at the right. Begin and end on *G*.

PERFORMANCE
Take turns playing your compositions for the class.

CHAPTER 3

THE NEW PITCH

Play each of the following patterns several times to become familiar with *D* and to learn how to move between pitches. HINT: A good sounding *D* requires even less air than *E*. Also, be sure to cover the holes completely with the flat area of your fingers, not the fingertips. Note that your right hand ring finger covers two small holes at the same time.

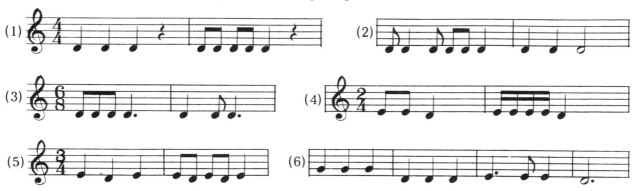

A Familiar Song - Duet

GETTING READY

Can you name this tune just by looking at the melody and thinking how it sounds?

Now play the melody on your recorder. Did you guess correctly?

Play the harmony part slowly.

PERFORMANCE

Divide into two groups and perform the duet. Switch parts and repeat.

Come, Let Us Gather

Traditional

GETTING READY

Practice the following patterns at a slow, steady tempo.

Sight read the entire song slowly.

PERFORMANCE

Perform the song in unison with guitar or piano accompaniment.

Divide into two groups and play the song as a two-part canon. (You may continue the accompaniment.)

Divide into three groups and play the song as a three-part canon.

Ode To Joy

L. van Beethoven

GETTING READY

You may be able to sight read Beethoven's melody without a mistake--try it.

PERFORMANCE

Play the song as written. If possible, breathe at the end of every four measures, not two. These are the phrase lengths Beethoven intended for his symphony's performance.

ENRICHMENT

Listen to the final movement of Beethoven's *Symphony No. 9*; you'll hear this melody.

John The Rabbit

American Folksong

Old John the rab-bit, oh yes, old John the rab-bit, oh yes, had a might-y bad hab-it,

oh yes, of go-in' to my gar-den, oh yes, and eat-in' up my peas, oh yes, and

cut-tin' down my cab-bage, oh yes, he ate to-ma-toes, oh yes, and sweet po-ta-toes,

oh yes, and if I live, oh yes, to see next fall, oh yes, then

I won't have oh yes, a gar-den at all! Oh yes!

RHYTHM TUTOR

= FERMATA

A **FERMATA** TELLS US TO INTERRUPT THE NORMAL TEMPO AND SUSTAIN THE PITCH UNDER THE FERMATA FOR A SPECIAL DRAMATIC EFFECT. THE LENGTH OF A FERMATA IS RELATIVE--NOT TOO LONG, NOT TOO SHORT--JUST LONG ENOUGH TO CREATE THE DESIRED EFFECT. TRY VARIOUS LENGTH FERMATAS AT THE END OF THIS SONG UNTIL YOU GET THE EMPHASIS YOU WANT.

GETTING READY

Your teacher will sing the song for you. You sing each *oh yes*.

As your teacher sings the song again, you play each *oh yes* on your recorder.

Divide into two groups. Group 1 sings the song (except for the *oh yes* responses). Group 2 plays each *oh yes* on recorders. Trade parts.

Your teacher will play the song on recorder. You play each *oh yes* on recorder. NOTE: When you learn to play *F-sharp* in the next chapter, you can play the song on recorder too.

PERFORMANCE

Decide on a form and perform the song.

Canon

T. Tallis

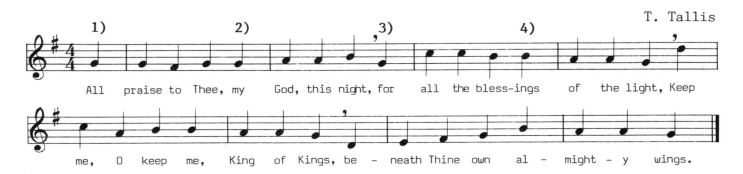

All praise to Thee, my God, this night, for all the bless-ings of the light, Keep
me, O keep me, King of Kings, be - neath Thine own al - might - y wings.

FORM TUTOR

IN A **CANON** ONE GROUP BEGINS. WHEN THIS GROUP REACHES THE PLACE IN
THE MUSIC MARKED WITH A 2), A SECOND GROUP BEGINS. SINCE THIS IS A
FOUR-PART CANON, THE SONG BEGINS FOUR TIMES WITH FOUR GROUPS. ONCE
A GROUP BEGINS, IT COMPLETES THE SONG.

THE FOLLOWING EXAMPLE SHOWS HOW EACH OF THE FOUR GROUPS BEGINS, BASED
ON THE LOCATION OF THE FOUR ENTRANCE NUMBERS IN THE MUSIC.

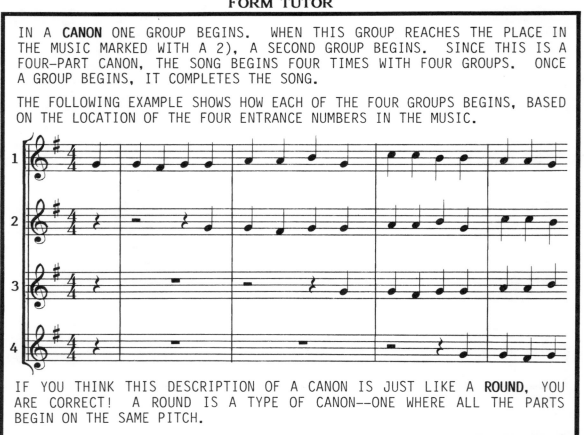

IF YOU THINK THIS DESCRIPTION OF A CANON IS JUST LIKE A **ROUND**, YOU
ARE CORRECT! A ROUND IS A TYPE OF CANON--ONE WHERE ALL THE PARTS
BEGIN ON THE SAME PITCH.

GETTING READY

Sight read the song, playing in **unison**--everyone plays the same part simultaneously.

Divide into four groups and practice just the four entrances, reading from the tutor.

PERFORMANCE

Divide into two groups and perform the canon in two parts (1 and 2). You may shorten
the last note of each phrase in order to breathe without changing the steady tempo.

Divide into three groups and perform the canon in three parts (1, 2, and 3).

Divide into four groups and perform the canon in four parts (1, 2, 3, and 4).

ENRICHMENT

Perform the composition as a combination vocal/recorder canon. For example, sing
parts 1 and 3, play parts 2 and 4.

Standin' On The Platform

North Carolina Folksong

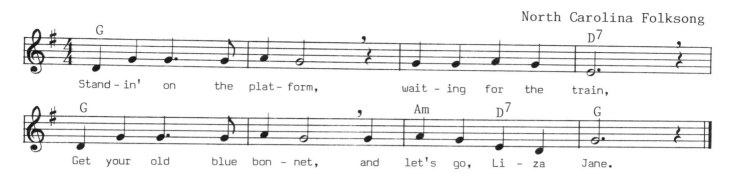

Stand-in' on the plat-form, wait-ing for the train,

Get your old blue bon-net, and let's go, Li-za Jane.

GETTING READY

Practice the following patterns:

Play each phrase of the song.

PERFORMANCE

Perform the song in this form: A (sing) A' (recorder) A" (sing with recorder). Add piano or guitar accompaniment if you wish.

ENRICHMENT

Add a cabasa or sand blocks playing ♩♩♩♩♩♩ rhythm plus a toy train whistle at the end of measures 4 and 8.

Cotton Eye Joe

Tennessee Folksong

Where did you come from? Where will you go? Where did you come from, Cot-ton eye Joe?

GETTING READY

Practice the following patterns:

Slowly sight read the song.

PERFORMANCE

Perform the song with an A A' form.

ENRICHMENT

Add this percussion accompaniment:

Add this second verse if you sing the song:
Come for to see you, come for to sing,
Come for to give you a diamond ring.

We Three Kings

Traditional Carol

METER TUTOR

THE $\frac{3}{8}$ TIME SIGNATURE TELLS YOU THERE WILL BE 3 BEATS PER MEASURE WITH AN EIGHTH NOTE OR REST RECEIVING ONE BEAT.   THIS IS A **TRIPLE METER.**

GETTING READY

Practice these patterns from the song:

Slowly sight read the song.

PERFORMANCE

Play the carol with piano or guitar accompaniment.

Down Came A Lady

Traditional

GETTING READY

Practice the following patterns. Be sure to keep a steady beat; each pattern will go faster than the previous one because the note values are shorter.

PERFORMANCE

Perform the song with an A A' A form.

ENRICHMENT

Add this ostinato to the arrangement:

Extend the lyrics of the song by creating additional lines, such as:

Down came two ladies, down came three . . . You complete the verse.

Compose a new melody for a B section using any of the notes in the song--*B*, *G*, *E*, or *D*. Begin and end on *G*. Your new B section can be for either voices or recorders. Here is a sample rhythm and text for you. Use your own if you feel creative.

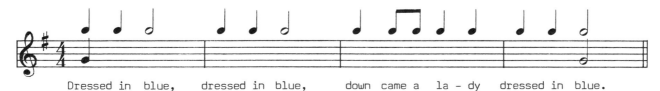

Perform the song in this form:
A   sing verse
B   one student plays her/his new melody on recorder
A'   sing verse (change color or entire verse for variety)
C   another student plays her/his new melody on recorder
A"   sing verse
D   a third student plays her/his new melody on recorder
A   sing and play verse 1
NOTE: A sections may be played and new sections may be sung.

FORM TUTOR

WHEN WE ALTERNATE THE ORIGINAL A SECTION WITH DIFFERENT CONTRASTING SECTIONS (A B A C A D A ETC.) WE MAKE **RONDO FORM.**

Old Paint

Western American Folksong

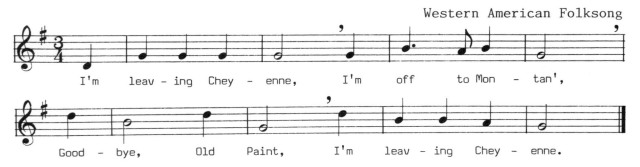

GETTING READY
Practice these two motives from the song.

Sight read the song.

PERFORMANCE
Perform the song with this form:
A (sing) A' (recorder) A" (both).

ENRICHMENT
Add this percussion accompaniment:

Old Dance Tune

German Folksong

GETTING READY
Practice these patterns from the song:

Sight read the song. Note that measures 2 and 4 of each section are the same.

PERFORMANCE
Play the song as written.

Divide recorders into two groups. Group 1 plays the first time, group 2 the second time through each section.

ENRICHMENT
Add this percussion accompaniment:

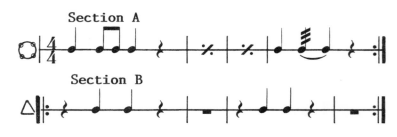

Tom Dooley

American Folksong

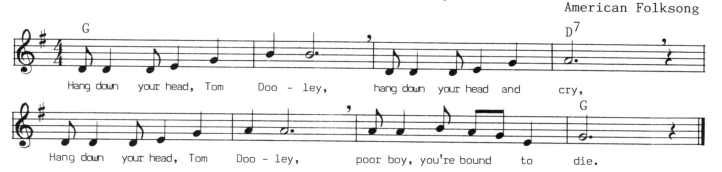

Hang down your head, Tom Doo - ley, hang down your head and cry,

Hang down your head, Tom Doo - ley, poor boy, you're bound to die.

GETTING READY

Practice these two patterns slowly, then a little faster.

Locate these rhythms in the song and play each complete phrase.

Sight read the song slowly.

PERFORMANCE

Perform the song with an A A' form.

MELODY TUTOR

 = PENTATONIC SCALE

A **SCALE** IS ANY SERIES OF PITCHES THAT CAN BE USED TO MAKE MELODIES.
A **PENTATONIC SCALE** USES FIVE PITCHES (PENTA). TONIC MEANS THAT THE
PITCHES ARE FOCUSED AROUND A CENTRAL OR HOME TONE. THIS PARTICULAR
SCALE IS THE **G PENTATONIC**. THOUSANDS OF MELODIES ARE BASED ON THE
PITCHES OF PENTATONIC SCALES.

Jingle Bells

American Carol

GETTING READY

You certainly know how this tune goes! Practice it slowly enough to articulate the rhythms cleanly at a steady tempo.

PERFORMANCE

Play the tune with piano accompaniment--sleigh bells too if they are handy.

Rainbow Song

Carol King*

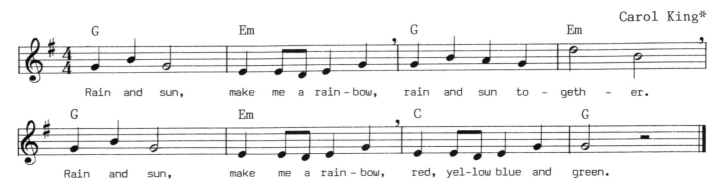

Rain and sun, make me a rain-bow, rain and sun to - geth - er.

Rain and sun, make me a rain-bow, red, yel-low blue and green.

RHYTHM TUTOR

> ▬ = HALF REST
>
> WHEN A TIME SIGNATURE HAS A 4 ON THE BOTTOM, A **HALF REST** GETS TWO SILENT BEATS. WHEN A TIME SIGNATURE HAS A 2 ON THE BOTTOM, A HALF REST GETS JUST ONE SILENT BEAT.

GETTING READY

Slowly sight read the song.   *Used by permission.

PERFORMANCE

Perform the song with an A (sing) A' (recorders) form. Add piano or guitar.

ENRICHMENT

Perform as above, but add one finger cymbal sound each time *rain* is sung, a suspended cymbal (soft mallet) each time *sun* is sung, and a chime bar when the song is over.

Improvisation - 2

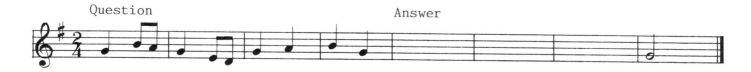

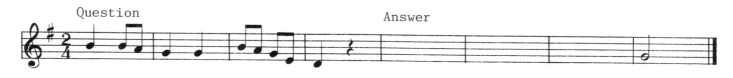

GETTING READY

Review the procedures outlined on page 9 for *Improvisation-1*. Use the same improvisation process again, but now you have five pitches to select from--*B*, *A*, *G*, *E*, *D*. These are the pitches of the *G pentatonic* scale. In order to bring your answers to a complete-sounding close, we suggest that you end on *G*.

PERFORMANCE

Here is a brief summary of the four steps from page 9:
(1) Answer with the same rhythm as the question; first motive may use same pitches.
(2) Change some of the rhythms in your answer.
(3) Perform your answer as a solo or as part of a duet or trio.
(4) Make up a new answer with some different pitches or rhythms.

Kansas Boys

American Folksong

GETTING READY

Chant the verse in rhythm, no pitches.

Clap the rhythm without the words.

Slowly play the song. You'll probably have to play slower than you just clapped! Practice until you can play the song up to tempo.

PERFORMANCE

Perform the song with an A (sing) A' (recorders) form.

ENRICHMENT

Make up a body instrument rhythm pattern to accompany the song. You might use hand claps, hand claps with a partner, finger snaps, thigh pats, or foot stamps.

Substitute other states and foods for additional verses.

Add the following percussion accompaniment to the song.

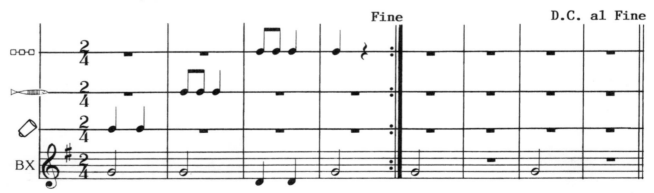

What You Gonna Call Your Pretty Little Baby?

African American Spiritual

What you gon-na call   your pret-ty lit-tle ba-by?   What you gon-na call   your pret-ty lit-tle

ba-by?   What you gon-na call   your pret-ty lit-tle ba-by?   Born, born in Beth-le-hem.

RHYTHM TUTOR

 = TIE

A **TIE** COMBINES THE VALUES OF TWO NOTES INTO ONE LONGER NOTE. IN THIS SONG AN EIGHTH NOTE (½ BEAT) IS TIED TO A HALF NOTE (2 BEATS) SO THE TOTAL VALUE OF THE TIED NOTES IS TWO AND A HALF BEATS.

GETTING READY

Practice the following patterns. Note that pattern 3, the final measure of the song, creates a new type of syncopated rhythm--two consecutive off-beat notes.

Play each phrase of the song slowly.

PERFORMANCE

Divide into three recorder groups, one for each of the first three phrases. Everyone plays the final phrase. Perform the song in an A (sing) A' (recorders) form.

ENRICHMENT

Perform the song as before, but add a glockenspiel playing phrase 4 as an introduction and an interlude between sections A and A'. Also add a finger cymbal on the first beat of each phrase and a chime bar during the final two measures.

Add the following piano accompaniment to the song:

Tutoring Tooters

Traditional

Section A

A tutor who tooted the flute *

Tried to tutor two tooters to toot *

Said the two to the tutor,

"Is it harder to toot,

Or to tutor two tooters to toot?" *

Section B

Group 1

Group 2

GETTING READY

Speak the rhyme using $\frac{6}{8}$ meter. Here is a possible way to speak line 1 for starters:

Speak the rhyme again and add a thigh pat (patsch) on each underlined syllable, a hand clap on each curly line syllable, and a foot stamp on each asterisk.

Substitute unpitched percussion instruments of your choice for the three body instruments and say the verse again with these new sounds.

Divide into two groups and slowly sight read section B on recorders.

PERFORMANCE

Perform the book's namesake song with this form:

A   speak rhyme
B   play on recorders in two groups
A'   speak poem with percussion instruments as marked
B'   play on recorders (trade parts)
A"   only instruments play (think the rhyme but say nothing)

Tennessee

VERSE
Tennessee Folksong

Wish I was in Ten-nes-see sit-tin' in an eas-y chair, My true love a-

long my side, a-comb-ing her love-ly hair. I shoo, oh la-dy, shoo, I

shoo, oh la-dy shy, Shoo, oh la-dy shoo, my love, and I'm go-in' to Ten-nes-see.

FORM TUTOR

MANY LONGER SONGS CONTAIN TWO CONTRASTING SECTIONS. OFTEN THESE ARE **VERSE – REFRAIN** SONGS. THE VERSE CHANGES TEXT WITH EACH REPETITION; THE REFRAIN REPEATS THE TEXT EACH TIME.

GETTING READY

Practice the following patterns. Note that patterns 5 and 6 were used in *John The Rabbit*, page 24. Remembering the rhythm from that song will help you learn *Tennessee*.

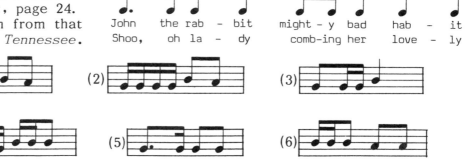

John the rab-bit   might-y bad   hab-it
Shoo, oh la-dy   comb-ing her   love-ly

(1) (2) (3)

(4) (5) (6)

Play the entire song slowly.

PERFORMANCE

Perform the song in this form: AB (sing) AB' (recorder) AB" (sing and recorders).

ENRICHMENT

Add this percussion ostinato to the arrangement:

A only

B only

A & B   BX

Create a new verse for the song. Here is a sample.
Wish I was in Tennessee, huntin' with my old dog Blue,
My true love along my side, watchin' for that possum stew.

CHAPTER 6

THE NEW PITCH

Practice each of the following patterns several times to become familiar with the new pitch and to learn how to move between pitches. This fourth line *D*, an **octave** higher than the *D* you learned in Chapter 3, is the first pitch that does not use a covered thumb hole. Move your left thumb slightly away from the thumb hole for this *D*. The slight downward pressure of your left hand middle finger and the slight upward pressure of the right thumb will balance the recorder.

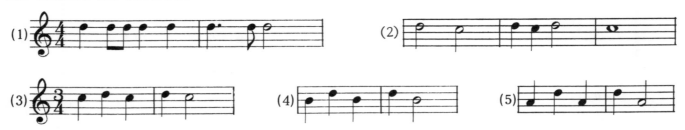

Good King Wenceslas

English Carol

GETTING READY

Here is a traditional carol that you probably know. Practice slowly; keep a steady beat.

PERFORMANCE

Rather than everyone playing the carol together, try a "pass the phrase" version. Begin at the back of the room--that person plays the first phrase. Then the next person plays a phrase and so on until everyone has played a phrase. This will take several repetitions of the carol. Everyone plays together to finish the carol if the last player stops in the middle.

CHAPTER 4

F sharp

THE NEW PITCH

Practice each of the following patterns several times to become familiar with the new pitch and to learn how to move between pitches. Be sure to cover the holes completely.

MELODY TUTOR

♯ = SHARP

WHEN A **SHARP** IS PLACED IN FRONT OF A NOTE, THE PITCH OF THAT NOTE IS RAISED BY A **HALF STEP**--TO THE NEXT POSSIBLE HIGHER PITCH. ALL REPETITIONS OF THE SAME NOTE IN THAT MEASURE ARE ALSO CHANGED.

MELODY TUTOR

= F-SHARP IN THE KEY SIGNATURE

YOU HAVE SEEN THE SHARP ON THE *F* LINE AT THE BEGINNING OF MANY SONGS. THIS **KEY SIGNATURE** TELLS US THAT ALL THE *F*s IN THE SONG SHOULD BE PLAYED AS *F-SHARP*, INCLUDING THOSE *F*s IN THE FIRST SPACE. WHENEVER AN *F-SHARP* IS IN THE KEY SIGNATURE, WE DO NOT NEED TO PLACE A SHARP IN FRONT OF EACH *F*.

Practice the following patterns. Remember that this key signature tells us that all the *F*s are *F-sharps*.

Play all of the pitches you have learned so far.

31

Hop-a-Doodle

American Folksong

Down in the mead - ow, hop-a-doo-dle, hop-a-doo-dle, down in the mead - ow
hop-a-doo-dle doo. Down in the mead - ow the colt be-gan to prance. The
cow be - gan to whis - tle and the pig be - gan to dance.

GETTING READY
Practice the following interval pattern.

Now play the pattern with different rhythms; first ♩ ♫ then ♫ ♫.

You have played all the different rhythm patterns and intervals in the song, so slowly sight read the entire song.

PERFORMANCE
Perform the song several times, each time a little faster. Alternate singing with recorder for an A A' form.

ENRICHMENT
Add this accompaniment to the song:

Rain On The Garden

S. McRae

Rain on the gar-den, rain on the tree, rain on the house-top but not on me.

GETTING READY

Speak the poem in rhythm, then slowly sight read the melody.

PERFORMANCE

Perform the song in a form of your choice.

BM

ENRICHMENT

Add the BM ostinato and also a different percussion instrument of your choice to play along on *garden*, *tree*, and *housetop*.

Pick any other rain rhyme (*Rain, Rain, Go Away*, for example) and improvise a penta-tonic melody (*D, E, G, A, B*) on recorder or mallet percussion. Use this as the B section of the song.

The Birch Tree

Russian Folksong

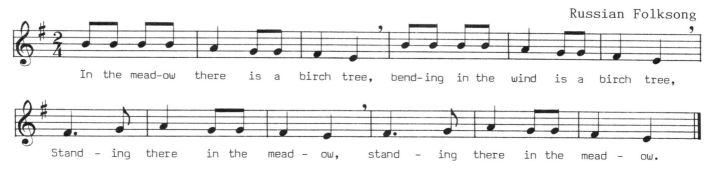

In the mead-ow there is a birch tree, bend-ing in the wind is a birch tree,

Stand - ing there in the mead - ow, stand - ing there in the mead - ow.

GETTING READY

Sight read the melody slowly, then increase the tempo on subsequent playings.

PERFORMANCE

Divide into two recorder groups. Group 1 plays phrases 1 and 3, group 2 plays phrases 2 and 4. Perform the song in an A (sing) A' (recorders) form.

ENRICHMENT

Add SG and AG to the melody on phrases 2 and 4, and add a brass chime rustle during phrases 1 and 3.

Add the following piano accompaniment to the arrangement.

Listen to the final movement of Tchaikovsky's *Symphony No. 4*, which uses this melody.

All Around The Butter Dish

Traditional Rhyme
Melody by S. McRae

GETTING READY

Speak the rhyme in rhythm. HINT: The rhythm of the first measure will remind you of skipping.

On recorders, play this rhythm on *G*:

Slowly play each line of the song.

Practice until you reach skipping tempo.

PERFORMANCE

Play the song as written.

ENRICHMENT

As a BX plays this ostinato,
△ plays on each circled word,
▱ plays on underlined syllables,
SG/AG play the pitches for boxed words.

Perform the song five times. All the instruments and recorders play the first time. The second time, recorders skip phrase one and enter on phrase two. Recorders wait an additional phrase on each subsequent repeat. By the fifth time, recorders don't play at all. The percussion instruments play each time.

Hey, Betty Martin

American Folksong

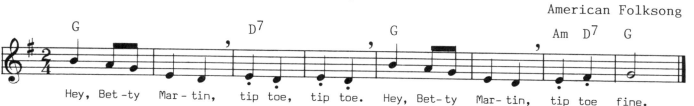

Hey, Bet-ty Mar-tin, tip toe, tip toe. Hey, Bet-ty Mar-tin, tip toe fine.

RHYTHM TUTOR

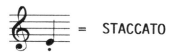 = STACCATO

THE DOTS BENEATH THE NOTE HEADS ARE **STACCATO** MARKS. THESE DOTS TELL US TO PLAY OR SING THE PITCHES IN A DETACHED MANNER. YOU WILL HAVE TO USE A *DUH...D, DUH...D* TONGUING BETWEEN EACH STACCATO NOTE RATHER THAN THE REGULAR *DUH... DUH...* ARTICULATION IN ORDER TO STOP THE AIR QUICKLY.

GETTING READY

Practice these patterns with regular articulation, then with **staccato** articulation. Be sure not to rush the tempo when you use staccato articulation.

Sight read the song slowly. Use the articulations shown.

PERFORMANCE

Perform the song with an A A' form. Use piano or guitar accompaniment if you wish.

ENRICHMENT

Add the following percussion ensemble to the arrangement. Perform the song in this form: A (sing) A' (recorder) A" (unpitched percussion) A"' (everything).

Chanson

French Folksong

Melody

Harmony

GETTING READY

Practice the following patterns slowly:

(1)   (2)

Practice each part of the duet slowly. Note that the phrases of the two lines overlap rather than coincide. This results in a smooth flow to the duet.

PERFORMANCE

Play the duet in this form: A (melody only) A' (harmony only) A" (both).

Rigaudon

H. Purcell

FORM TUTOR

FIRST ENDING   SECOND ENDING

FIRST AND **SECOND ENDINGS** ARE USED WHEN A SECTION IS TO BE REPEATED BUT THE ENDING OF EACH PART IS SLIGHTLY DIFFERENT. THE FIRST TIME THE SECTION IS PLAYED, THE **FIRST ENDING** IS USED. WHEN THE SECTION IS REPEATED, THE FIRST ENDING IS SKIPPED AND THE **SECOND ENDING** IS PLAYED. THE LENGTH OF EACH ENDING IS INDICATED BY THE BRACKET ABOVE THE MUSIC.

GETTING READY

Practice these patterns slowly to get used to the intervals and the two endings.

(1)   (2)

PERFORMANCE

Play the song as written.

Fais Do Do - Duet

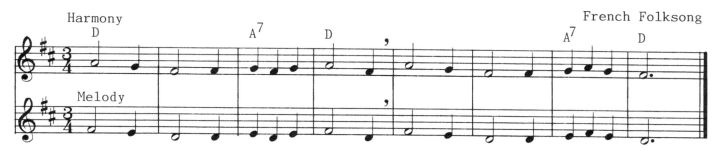

French Folksong

GETTING READY

This song should be familiar; you played it on page 4 using *B*, *A*, and *G*. That version of *Fais Do Do* was focused around the pitch *G*, which was the tonic. In this duet version *D* is the tonic.

Practice the following patterns.

Sight read the melody of the song.

Sight read the harmony line of the song. You will note that the harmony has the same melodic contour as the melody. This is called **parallel harmony.**

PERFORMANCE

Divide into two recorder groups and play the tune with an A (melody) A' (melody with harmony) form. Play it again and switch parts.

Improvisation - 3

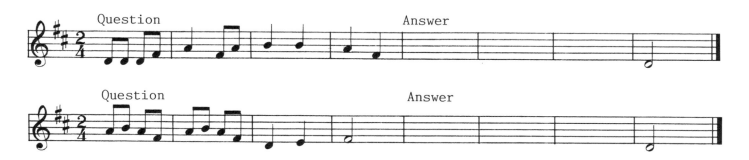

GETTING READY

Review the procedures outlined on page 9. Use this improvisation process again unless you want to try something new. For this improvisation use *D*, *E*, *F-sharp*, *A*, or *B*.

Boat Song

Nigerian Folksong

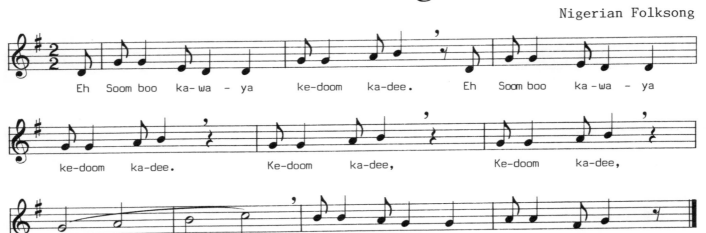

Eh Soom boo ka-wa - ya ke-doom ka-dee. Eh Soom boo ka-wa - ya
ke-doom ka-dee. Ke-doom ka-dee, Ke-doom ka-dee,
ah _____ Soom boo ka-wa - ya, ke-doom ka-dee.

GETTING READY

As you practice this lively syncopated rhythm, keep in mind the slow duple meter which might represent the paddle strokes. Play these rhythms on G.

Say the words of the song in rhythm.

Slowly sight read the melody.

PERFORMANCE

Perform the song with an A (sing) A' (recorders) form.

ENRICHMENT

Add these percussion ostinatos to the arrangement:

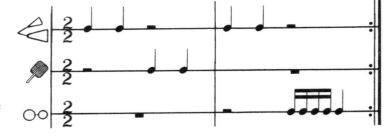

As a B section, divide into two groups and improvise question/answer phrases on hand drums--four measures each. Also, add an introduction--xylophones playing soft glissandos to suggest movement of the water.

Michael, Row The Boat Ashore

American Folksong

Mi - chael, row the boat a - shore, hal - le - lu - jah,

Mi - chael, row the boat a - shore, hal - le - lu - jah,

Mi - chael, row the boat a - shore, hal - le - lu - jah.

Mi - chael, row the boat a - shore, hal - le - lu - jah.

METER TUTOR

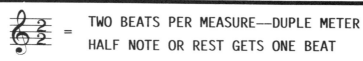 = TWO BEATS PER MEASURE—DUPLE METER

HALF NOTE OR REST GETS ONE BEAT

IT IS EASY TO ASSUME THAT HALF NOTES ALWAYS RECEIVE TWO BEATS. THEY DO WHENEVER THE TIME SIGNATURE HAS A 4 ON THE BOTTOM. BUT WHEN A 2 IS ON THE BOTTOM, A HALF NOTE RECEIVES JUST ONE BEAT.

RHYTHM TUTOR

𝅝 = WHOLE NOTE

IN 2/2 MUSIC A **WHOLE NOTE** RECEIVES 2 BEATS; IN 4/4 MUSIC IT RECEIVES 4 BEATS. IN EITHER CASE, THE WHOLE NOTE LASTS FOR A WHOLE MEASURE.

GETTING READY

Slowly practice each phrase of the melody as you feel four beats per measure. Be sure to play the song as written, not as you might have learned it.

Slowly practice each phrase of the harmony.

Divide into two groups and slowly play both lines of music together. On subsequent playings, gradually increase the tempo until you feel the music comfortably in duple meter.

PERFORMANCE

Play just the melody with an A (sing) A' (recorders) form. Add guitar or piano.

Perform the song with an A (recorder melody) A' (recorder melody and harmony) form.

Perform the song with an A (sing melody) A' (sing melody, recorder harmony) form.

Chanson à Deux

French Folksong

GETTING READY
Practice the melody line slowly.

PERFORMANCE
Play the melody of the duet as your teacher plays the parallel harmony line. In a few more chapters, you will be able to play the harmony line. Add guitar or piano if you wish.

ENRICHMENT
Play the melody twice on recorder as your teacher plays the following "music box" accompaniment and a volunteer plays the triangle part. Another volunteer, on guiro, gets to improvise winding the music box at the beginning. Your teacher will gradually slow down as you play, then stop, at which time the guiro player winds the music box again. Everyone finishes the song at tempo.

Kum Ba Yah

African Folksong

GETTING READY

Practice the following patterns slowly. Don't forget, a tie combines the rhythm values of the two notes connected by the tie into one longer note.

Play each phrase of the melody by itself. When you are secure with each phrase, combine two phrases, then three phrases; finally play the whole song.

PERFORMANCE

Perform the song with this form: A (sing) A' (recorder) A" (both). Accompany with piano or guitar.

ENRICHMENT

Sing additional verses, alternating them with recorder.

Someone's praying, Lord . . .
Someone's crying, Lord . . .

Bransle

C. Gervaise

GETTING READY

By now you are becoming a competent performer and musician. Slowly sight read this tune to prove it.

PERFORMANCE

Increase the speed to a walking tempo for the performance.

ENRICHMENT

Suggest one or more percussion ostinatos you think would enhance the song. Your teacher will help you notate your sounds. Add these to the arrangement.

Miss Mary Mack

Children's Street Game

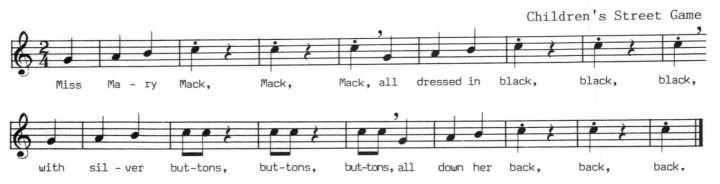

GETTING READY

Sight read the song, then wait for the fun to start!

PERFORMANCE

Sit or stand in a circle. One person plays the first phrase, *Miss Mary Mack*. Keeping the tempo, the next person to the right plays the next *Mack*, and the third person to the right plays the third *Mack*. The fourth person plays *all dressed in black*, and the answer *black, black* is passed farther to the right, one person at a time. Keep moving around the circle in this fashion. The song should be repeated two or three times, each time faster.

For variety the lead person sings the phrase and the two answering persons play the answer on recorder.

All Through The Night

Welsh Folksong

Section A

Section B

Melody

Harmony

FORM TUTOR

D.C. al FINE

D.C. IS THE ABBREVIATION FOR *DA CAPO* (DAH COP-O), THE ITALIAN TERM FOR "FROM THE TOP," THAT IS, "RETURN TO THE BEGINNING."

FINE (FEE NAY) IS THE ITALIAN TERM FOR "THE END." **D.C. al FINE** MEANS TO PLAY THE MUSIC AGAIN FROM THE BEGINNING, BUT STOP AT THE *FINE*. REPEATS ARE NOT NORMALLY TAKEN AFTER A *D.C.*

TO REVIEW, THE ROADSIGNS IN THIS PIECE TELL US TO
    PLAY THE A SECTION, THEN REPEAT IT,
    PLAY THE B SECTION THEN RETURN TO THE BEGINNING,
    PLAY THE A SECTION ONE TIME AND STOP AT THE *FINE*.

GETTING READY

Sight read each phrase of the melody at a slow tempo. Keep the beat steady and make sure you sustain the long notes full value.

PERFORMANCE

Play the melody in section A and the harmony in Section B. Your teacher will play the B section melody. In a few weeks (Chapter 8) you will be able to play the entire melody.

CHAPTER 5

THE NEW PITCH

Practice each of the following patterns several times to become familiar with the new pitch and to learn how to move between pitches. Use the right thumb to help balance the recorder.

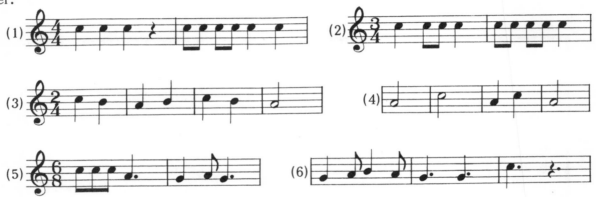

Peas Porridge Still Hot

Traditional

GETTING READY

Here is a new melody for our very first song. Practice slowly with a steady beat.

PERFORMANCE

Play the song with piano or guitar accompaniment. Add the lyrics if you wish.

ENRICHMENT

You have now played two versions of this verse. Why not make up a third version? Keep the same rhythm, but use any of the seven pitches you can now play. Begin and end on *G*.

Fair Delona

Arabian Folksong

GETTING READY

Practice each of the following patterns slowly.

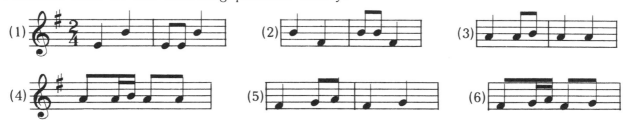

Practice each phrase of the song slowly.   Note the unusual three measure phrases.

PERFORMANCE

Play the song three to five times, each time a little faster.

ENRICHMENT

Perform the song with the following percussion accompaniment:

Au Clair De La Lune

French Folksong

GETTING READY

Practice each phrase slowly. At practice tempos you may need additional breaths. Review the musical roadsigns on page 37.

PERFORMANCE

Play the song on recorders as written. NOTE: The design of this song is the same as it was for *All Through The Night*. But since each segment of *Au Clair De La Lune* is only one phrase long, the entire piece is considered to be a single A section with a phrase design of **a a b a.**

ENRICHMENT

Perform the song with the following accompaniment: